# A World According to God

· · · · · · · · · · · · · · · · · · · · · · · · · · · · · · · · ·

Martha Ellen Stortz

Foreword by Ron Hansen

# A World According to God

· · · · · · · · · · · · · · · · · · · · · · · · · · · · · · · ·

## Practices for Putting Faith at the Center of Your Life

JOSSEY-BASS
A Wiley Imprint
www.josseybass.com

Published by Jossey-Bass
A Wiley Imprint
989 Market Street, San Francisco, CA 94103–1741   www.josseybass.com

Jossey-Bass books and products are available through most bookstores. To contact Jossey-Bass directly, call our Customer Care Department within the United States at (800) 956-7739, outside the United States at (317) 572-3986 or fax (317) 572-4002.

Jossey-Bass also publishes its books in a variety of electronic formats. Some content that appears in print may not be available in electronic books.

**Library of Congress Cataloging-in-Publication Data**

Stortz, Martha Ellen, date.
  A world according to God : practices for putting faith at the center
of your life / Martha Ellen Stortz ; foreword by Ron Hansen.
       p. cm.
Includes bibliographical references and index.
ISBN 0-7879-5981-2 (alk. paper)
  1. Christian life—Meditations.  I. Title.
BV4501.3.S763 2004
248.4—dc22

                                          2003021183

Printed in the United States of America
FIRST EDITION
HB Printing          10 9 8 7 6 5 4 3 2 1

# Contents

• • • • • • • • • • • • • • • • • • • • • • • • • • • • • • • • • •

# Foreword

E ver since Jesus was lifted up from the mount called Olivet, his disciples have endeavored to find a way of life in the world that
would be a perfect imitation of his own. We read in Acts that Peter,
filled with the Holy Spirit, baptized three thousand converts on the
day of Pentecost, and "they devoted themselves to the apostles' teaching and fellowship, to the breaking of bread and the prayers. . . .
All who believed were together and had all things in common; they
would sell their possessions and goods and distribute the proceeds to
all, as any had need."

But Acts soon becomes a book describing persecution and dis-
sension rather than a heavenly kingdom on earth. Stephen is
stoned, James is killed, and Peter and Paul imprisoned; there are hot
disputes about eating forbidden foods, about including gentiles in
their group, about the handling of alms for widows and orphans, and
whether males were required to be circumcised. The slogan "What
Would Jesus Do?" could have originated then, as the heroic, floun-
dering, holy, fractious Christian religion gradually came into being.

In fact, there seems to have been no idyllic time for the faithful
who followed the one known as *Christós*. With each gain in worldly
acceptance, assets, prestige, and suzerainty, there seemed to be con-
sequent losses in fidelity to the gospel Jesus preached. And there
was always someone to famously protest the Christian world's latest failure and inconstancy, whether it was Anthony and his retreat

ix
. . .

into a hermit's life in fourth-century Egypt, Clare of Assisi and her example of chastity, poverty, and simplicity in an age of religious scandal, greediness, and pomp, or an affronted Martin Luther and the revolution he initiated upon fastening his ninety-five theses on the front door of All Saints Church in Wittenberg. The history is stormy, and the factions and rivalries within Christian denominations today are only a little less tempestuous than when nations stubbornly took stands over the creedal formula "one in being with the father."

It may ever be so. *Ecclesia semper reformanda*—the Church must always be reformed—is a persistent reminder that ethical consistency, personal sacrifice, and heartfelt adherence to the norms and commands of Jesus of Nazareth are difficult for humans and their institutions, for, as Dietrich Bonhoeffer wrote in *The Cost of Discipleship,* "When Christ calls a man, he bids him come and die."

Embracing the Cross seldom means martyrdom now, but there are probably no Christians who will not experience some form of shame and rejection in their lives. In our passage through hardships, despair, and feelings of lonely trial and failure, however, we have help and companionship in what Stortz refers to as "the core practices of the Christian faith."

"Baptism," she writes, "inaugurates the journey; the Lord's Supper provides food and drink; prayer connects us to the one whom we follow; forgiveness allows us to go forward together; remembering the dead offers us the counsel of the saints who have gone before; and fidelity makes community possible in the first place."

We are not in this alone. An associate of mine was in the seminary, unhappy in his circumstances, and prepared to call it quits. With his trunk packed, he sat on it and offered Christ a prayer of explanation, saying, "I just can't do this without a friend." But he heard an interior voice quietly ask, "Can I be that friend?" And he stayed the course. As Stortz points out here, "Discipleship is first and foremost the journey into a relationship that deepens and grows."

John Irving's *The World According to Garp* was a best-selling comic novel about the bizarre adventures of a young T. S. Garp, who is striving after wisdom and a utopia for his family in the midst of chaos, fatality, and mutilation. In *A World According to God*, Stortz plays on that title to picture how the world would look if framed by the core practices of Christian faith—if, in fact, the peaceable kingdom of God that Jesus urged on his hearers was given its rightful preeminence. Writing on the Lord's Supper, Stortz imagines a far different social reality than the culture of death and seeming meaninglessness that Irving satirized and that we have learned to tolerate. She sees instead a reconciled, grace-filled creation "pointing us all toward a final banquet when all the children of the world sit at table and break bread and drink wine together. Eucharistic living nurtures disciples in the meantime, teaching them to move through the world with open hands, as we give and receive both blessings and bread."

On the night he died, Swiss theologian Karl Barth was scratching out a lecture in which he stated, "God is not a God of the dead but of the living." The fullest implication of Karl Barth's thought is that the shabbiness, messiness, and errors and omissions to which we are subject have not just earned us God's pity but God's everlasting love. Writing on Wolfgang Amadeus Mozart, Karl Barth noted that "What occurs in Mozart is rather a glorious upsetting of the balance, a turning in which the light rises and the shadows fall, though without disappearing, in which joy overtakes sorrow without extinguishing it, in which the Yea rings louder than the ever-present Nay."

So it is in *A World According to God*. The imitation of Christ that is the call of discipleship upsets the status quo. It is to become aware of a world made strange by seeing things as Christ did. Imitation means faith practices such as "relinquishing the old," practicing "steady and intentional acts of kindness, generosity, beauty," "paying attention" to the many, nuanced incarnations of God in the vagaries of our haphazard lives.

Stortz writes of Saint Francis of Assisi that, "In his interactions with the poor and outcast, in his great delight in the spectrum of God's creation, even in his gentle teasing about human failings, Francis radiated the Good News. 'Preach the Gospel without ceasing,' he is reported to have said. 'Use words if necessary.'"

*A World According to God* preaches the Gospel with affability, intimacy, wisdom, and necessary words of challenge, counsel, and healing. It is a book to be grateful for.

Ron Hansen

# Acknowledgments

· · · · · · · · · · · · · · · · · · · · · · · · · · · · · · · ·

W riting is its own pilgrimage. Happily, the journey is a crowded one. The path that led to this book was peopled with friends and colleagues. Their voices cheered me when I locked myself away to write.

Two people deserve particular thanks. Sheryl Fullerton, senior editor at Jossey-Bass, had a steady and sure compass for this project, and she signaled the way ahead when I could not discern it myself. She invited the preacher's voice into my scholarly prose, pointing me toward insight and illustration rather than my usual documentation with all manner of supporting evidence.

My husband and on-site editor, William Spohn, provided unfailing cheer, abundant distraction, and conversation that kept us at table long into the night. Talking to Bill always offered the jolt of adrenaline that sent me back to my work enthused and energized. He is himself a writer and teacher, but more than both, he counts himself a disciple. He has been at my side every step of the way, and he continues to accompany me in the journey of marriage.

I am grateful for the hearty camaraderie of a group of faculty women colleagues at the Graduate Theological Union: Margaret R. Miles, Barbara Green, Sandra Schneiders, and Gina Hens-Piazza. Team-teaching with colleague and friend Richard M. Gula afforded yet another opportunity for exploring spiritual practice. Students in our courses "The Moral Imagination" and "Spirituality and Ethics" sharpened our focus as they shared their own stories from the journey of discipleship. My colleague in liturgics Michael B. Aune and I collaborated in a course titled "Praise, Action, and Agency," which worked consciously on the interface between faith practices and the moral life. Later, students at my own seminary would approach me to do a course on Dietrich Bonhoeffer. Together we studied the "rule" Bonhoeffer wrote for his own community at Finkenwalde, *Life Together*, and we used the practices he outlined there.

The late Timothy F. Lull, former president and dean of Pacific Lutheran Theological Seminary, urged me to probe my own Lutheran tradition more deeply for insight into the relationship between spirituality and ethics, and his lively intellect remains an enduring influence on my work. An invitation to offer the Hein-Fry Lectures, sponsored by the Evangelical Lutheran Church in America, in 1998 gave me an opportunity to connect core faith practices with pressing contemporary moral concerns, and I probed Martin Luther's insights on baptism for their counsel on dying and his teaching on the Lord's Supper for its wisdom on poverty and hunger. Work with other Lutheran ethicists on a collection of essays for *The Promise of Lutheran Ethics* (Fortress, 1998) pushed me to articulate a Protestant spirituality that did not fall prey to "works-righteousness." I owe thanks to the other authors for their own critical appropriation of a rich tradition: Robert Benne, James M. Childs Jr., Richard J. Perry Jr., Cynthia Moe-Lobeda, Larry Rasmussen, David Fredrickson, John Stumme, and Karen Bloomquist. Finally, many others shepherded this work through ongoing friendship and collegiality. They may not remember the circumstances or the conversations, but I do, and I thank in particular Dorothy Bass, Bonnie Miller-McLemore, Catherine Wallace, Diane Jacobson, Clare B. Fischer, Margaret R. Miles, Gary Simpson, Lois Malcolm, Christian Scharen, Timothy Sedgwick, Vigen Guroian, and Susan K. Wood.

I would be remiss if I did not thank all the regulars at Montclair Swim Club, some of whom find "a practicing Christian" something of a curiosity. Nonetheless, we all share stories, jokes, and general banter, and their company warms the icy waters of the pool.

Only some of the companions along the way can be named. Others remain nameless, but a question they raised after a lecture or sermon haunted me for weeks. I am grateful for speaking invitations that forced me to refine my thoughts: the Yost Lectures in 1996 at Lutheran Theological Southern Seminary in Columbia, South Carolina; the Hein-Fry Lectures in 1998 at Luther Seminary, Lutheran Theological Southern Seminary, Gettysburg Theological Seminary, and Pacific Lutheran Theological Seminary; the Graduate Theological Union's distinguished faculty lecture for 1998; the Mid-Winter Convocation at Roanoke College in Salem, Virginia, in 2002. In addition, I road-tested the material for this book at countless pastors' retreats, professional leadership gatherings, and congregations around the country. As I have walked up and down in the church, I find people who know these practices in their bones. Again and again, their wisdom blessed me.

Finally, I am grateful for all the opportunities I have had to preach in my own seminary community. It is a gift and a challenge to bring into conversation scripture's deepest knowing and the world's most intractable problems. I thank the students, staff, and faculty colleagues who gather to worship and pray and read the Bible together. In addition to the seminary community, I am happy to be part of the early morning Mass crowd at Holy Spirit Parish in Berkeley, where my Roman Catholic husband regularly worships. When my own resources ran dry, I found refreshment in corporate worship and in the practices described here.

M.E.S.

# A World According to God

# Imagining a World According to God

At a summer picnic, a four-year-old boy solemnly passes a plate of raw vegetables to his father with the words, "A carrot, Daddy, given for you."

I wheel my mother-in-law around the halls of a nursing home. She does not recognize me this time, and her conversation follows a logic increasingly difficult to discern. But as we follow the long hallways around, we sing the first two verses of the hymn "Love Divine, All Loves Excelling." She summons the words from a part of her brain as yet untouched by this ravaging disease, and they come readily to her lips. The lilting melody of the hymn comforts us both.

My urban parish hosts its monthly Loaves and Fishes dinner. From all corners of the city, forty-odd homeless men, women, and children gather for a meal cooked and served by a team of parishioners. As they sit at linen-covered tables lit by candles, these people shed the labels they bear on the streets—"welfare queens," "clients," or "urban blight"—and become honored guests.

A woman turns on the evening news to hear of the Columbine High School shooting. Images of terrified students pouring from campus buildings flicker across the screen. From the audio feed the sound of gunfire fills the darkened living room. The woman sinks leadenly into the couch and makes the sign of the cross.

A family picnic, a visit to a nursing home, a soup kitchen, the evening news: these are snapshots from ordinary life. Each of these snapshots draws on a core practice in the Christian tradition. Asked to pass the carrots, a young boy instinctively makes a connection to another meal closely observed. In a parish hall around candlelit tables, parishioners look at the same eucharistic meal and see in it a dimension of radical hospitality. The visit to a relative with Alzheimer's becomes the occasion of praise-making. A woman supplies the gesture of redemption a tragedy cries out for. The practices of discipleship reframe ordinary life.

For centuries Christians have sung hymns, gathered at table, and offered prayer to God. Practices like prayer, praise, and table fellowship are too lively to be locked down in worship services; they burst out of liturgical boxes. Writer Annie Dillard hints at the power that practices bear: "I often think of the set pieces of liturgy as certain words which people have successfully addressed to God without their getting killed."[1] Dillard's insight strikes home. These timeworn and tradition-honored practices of the faith crackle with energy.

I want to gather these snapshots into an album with the title "A World According to God" because I am convinced that these core practices are neither random acts nor ritual tics. They are more like eye exercises, designed to correct and strengthen weak vision. Doing them over time and in community, we learn to see things from a God's-eye view. We come to know the world according to God.

This book is for all those disciples who long for a glimpse of God's world. It is time to rediscover the power in these core practices of practicing Christians. Practices of discipleship place our lives in a new context. *What we do* in those practices informs what we do in the crises great and small that intrude unbidden into daily life. These core faith practices shape us in ways that directly influence how we negotiate everyday life. They have everything to do with the moral life, if we could but pause to make the connections. This book offers that pause by addressing three questions at the outset: Why do practices afford us a glimpse of the world according to God? What are practices anyway? What do they do to us?

## Disciplines of Disciples

The Christian faith is not primarily about doctrines that tell us what to believe, nor is it about rules that tell us what to do. Certainly, doctrines and deeds matter, but what matters most is following Jesus. The Christian faith grows out of an encounter with the risen Lord.

This is very different from religions that organize themselves around commitment to a cause or belief in a set of abstract ideas. These religions create adepts or devotees or adherents. In contrast, Christianity distinctively names its followers "disciples." Personal relationship to the risen Christ sustains Christian discipleship. The faith practices of Christianity develop as disciples seek to stay close to the One whom they love, the One whom they follow. A psychotherapist would probably regard these faith practices as exercises in building and sustaining intimacy. Christian disciples thus need to sustain their intimacy with the risen Christ. And as the disciplines of disciples, practices keep us in close proximity to him, allowing his presence to pattern our lives; they offer ways of acting out our relationship with Jesus; and they give us a view of the world from his perspective.

## Meeting Jesus Again for the First Time

In his teachings and healings, in his life and death and resurrection, in his dealings with rich and poor, Jew and Greek, woman and man, Jesus lived in a world according to God. We can see it still, if we stop to look. The disciplines of discipleship resurrect the view. Each of the core faith practices traces its origin back to the life of Jesus. Disciples do these things because he did them. They pray the way

Jesus taught them to pray: "Our Father, who art in heaven." Jesus forgave his disciples' disloyalty, and he asked them to forgive others' failings. He was baptized in the Jordan River, and he commissioned the disciples to baptize in his name. He asked the disciples to break bread and drink wine "in remembrance of me." The original disciples passed on the disciplines they had learned from their Lord. We do these things to remember him. As we remember, we "meet Jesus again for the first time."[2]

For Christians, the question "What would Jesus do?"—abbreviated on wristbands, T-shirts, and bumper stickers as "WWJD?"—is important but not primary. What animates discipleship and directs the way we live is not so much identifying what Jesus would do as "meeting him again" in daily life. Christian discipleship follows from encounters with the risen Lord.

Disciples reencounter Jesus in the practices he left behind: "For where two or three are gathered in my name, I am there among them" (Matthew 18:20). As we engage in the disciplines that Jesus himself did, we meet the risen Lord. Practices are places where Jesus promises to be. Luke's Gospel suggests this in its account of a postresurrection encounter. A stranger joins the disciples on the road to Emmaus, and he asks them about events that took place in the city of Jerusalem, specifically the crucifixion of the alleged King of the Jews. The stranger draws them into conversation about the scriptures, opening to them fresh interpretations. The disciples invite the man to dinner, but it is only in the breaking of the bread that they recognize him as the risen Christ (Luke 24:31). They have "met Jesus again." Just as the first disciples reencountered their beloved Lord at table, so we meet Jesus again whenever we gather to celebrate the Lord's meal, whenever we bow our heads in prayer or lift our voices in song. The risen Lord is present, and we meet him again for the first time.

Certainly these disciplines of discipleship are not the only places where Jesus walks in the world today. But if we recognize him in these practices, we will begin to see him in less obvious, more hidden places. One of my favorite preachers explains this process of recognition with an irreverent analogy: "To a pickpocket, all the world's a pocket!" He asks his listeners to think how sharply focused a pickpocket's eyes are on pockets with a slight bulge. The eyes of disciples, he implies, are focused differently. Practices train them on the One whom they follow. Having met Jesus again and again, disciples gradually discern his presence in all things. In his poem "As Kingfishers Catch Fire," nineteenth-century poet Gerard Manley Hopkins describes how the world looks to a disciple:

> For Christ plays in ten thousand places,
> Lovely in limbs, and lovely in eyes not his
> To the Father through the features of men's faces.[3]

## Acting Out Our Relationship to Jesus: Making His Gestures Our Own

As the vignettes at the beginning of this chapter demonstrate, faith practices are embodied actions, not abstract concepts. Practices require bodies, and disciples have them to offer. Jesus cared enough about bodies to spend much of his earthly ministry healing them and making them whole. Some of the best "teaching moments" in the Gospels happen when Jesus and his followers were hungry, angry, lonely, or falling asleep on their feet. Remember the feedings of the five thousand (Matthew 14:13–21; Mark 6:30–44; Luke 9:10–17; John 6:1–13), the woman who washed Jesus' feet with her tears, anointed them with fine oil, and dried them with her hair (Luke 7:36–50), or Jesus' long night of prayer in Gethsemane (Matthew 26:36–46; Mark 14:32–42; Luke 22:39–46). Bodies matter in the life of faith, and for that reason practices engage them.

But bodies matter because practices deal with basic human needs: the need to eat, the need to drink, the need for companionship, the need to listen, the need to mark and be marked as members of a particular group, and so on. Addressing these basic human needs, practices use the body to mentor the soul. Practices inscribe the encounter with Jesus on the body of the disciple. For example, Jews and Christians have sung or chanted psalms for centuries, often in an ancient call-and-response pattern. As a child, I was a member of the junior choir, and we routinely sang the introit and gradual, those scraps of psalms woven into the opening of the worship service. We were only in grade school, and we struggled with the strange cadences of old plainsong melodies and with the lost eloquence of the King James Version of the Bible, but these fragments of psalms remain with me. Decades later, I can resurrect a psalm simply by humming one of the plainsong settings. This practice of singing planted the psalms deep in my body.

## Seeing as Jesus Sees

Faith practices also refocus our vision. Christian practices invite us into the world Jesus traveled and enable us to see it through his eyes. Several cascading parables in Matthew's Gospel paint pictures in words. All begin with the same refrain: "The kingdom of heaven is like a mustard seed. The kingdom of heaven is like a treasure hidden in a field. The kingdom of heaven is like a merchant in search of fine pearls. The kingdom of heaven is like a net thrown into the sea" (Matthew 13:31–50). The people who listened to these parables knew a world of fields and seeds and fishing nets. They did not know God's kingdom, but fortified with these vivid images, they could begin to imagine it. In the word pictures, Jesus invited his disciples to connect the ordinary with the extraordinary, the known with the unknown, the visible with the invisible. The kingdom of heaven filtered down into their everyday lives, and Jesus' followers gradually gained a new way of looking at the world around them. The practice of reading and meditating on this string of parables helps us begin to see things as Jesus does; they offer a God's-eye view.

## God-Shaped and God-Shaping Activities

Faith practices are the disciplines of discipleship. We may at times do them by rote or routine, but they orient us to the journey of discipleship. We do not make the journey alone: we travel with a whole company of disciples from around the world and across the centuries. We do not make the journey without a map: practices orient us to the One whom we follow. In John's Gospel, Jesus promised to send the disciples the Holy Spirit. He did not leave them without comfort (John 14:18). Nor did Jesus leave them without compass. As they did for the first disciples, practices point us to the person we love and illumine the path we follow. Like the polestar, they show disciples the direction of "true" north.

Practices are God-shaped and God-shaping activities that form the way of life called discipleship.[4] Faith practices find their roots in the life of Jesus and their place in the world. For those wishing to become a part of the way of life called "Christian," faith practices describe the way of life that constitutes discipleship. Many Protestant traditions shy away from talk of "spiritual exercises" or "disciplines of discipleship." They fear that this constitutes "works righteousness," a code phrase for the idea that disciples must earn their way into heaven by doing good deeds or becoming saints. There was no greater enemy of "works righteousness" than Martin Luther. Yet again and again, Luther counseled his parishioners to practice their faith. He saw faith practices as "gifts" given by God to God's people—and he urged people to receive these gifts with delight. As God-shaped gifts, faith practices point us to where we can find the body of Christ in the world today.

Practices are not only God-shaped; they are also God-shaping. Practices shape us into being certain kinds of people; they confer identity, identifying us to ourselves and to others. Initiated by these practices into a certain way of life, we come to identify ourselves as people who do these kinds of things. For example, a friend is a writer, and he is a writer because he does the things that writers do.

He became a writer by writing in a disciplined way on a daily basis, whether he felt particularly inspired on that day or not. Some days the words simply would not come, and after five hours of work he had only a paragraph. On other days the paragraphs would roll out. Being away from his writing desk left him disoriented and grouchy. "Whether I'm churning out pages or not, being in front of the computer makes me feel like myself again." Writing identified him to himself.

Being a practicing Christian is like being a writer. I am a Christian, and part of the reason is that I do the things Christians do: show up in church, study scripture, pray for my neighbors. These are often not "mountaintop" experiences—in fact, they rarely are. More than doing something *for* me, engaging in these practices does something *to* me. They invite me to participate more deeply in the way of life called "Christian." Through practices, a tradition enters the heart; through practices, beliefs enter the body. Practices provide the soil for sustained religious experience.

These God-shaping practices not only identify us to ourselves but also identify us to others. Religious practices function as the public face of a tradition in the world. Campaigning for the civil rights of African Americans in the 1950s, Martin Luther King Jr. did not try to speak a religious Esperanto that would hide who he was or where he came from. He believed that racial discrimination ran against the grain of the biblical witness, and he was not afraid to say so. No one would have remembered words like: "I have an idea I'd kind of like to share with you." But it was more than an "idea"; it was a "dream," and behind that dream were words from the prophet Joel for those who had ears to hear:

> I will pour out my spirit on all flesh;
> your sons and your daughters shall prophesy,
> your old men shall dream dreams,
> and your young men shall see visions.
> Even on the male and female slaves,
> in those days, I will pour out my spirit [Joel 2:28–29].

Martin Luther King Jr. drew these distinctive images from the world he knew as a Christian. He spoke in his mother tongue, and he had a religiously tutored first language to use. That language expressed his deepest convictions. King did not talk about oppression in general or hope in the abstract. Rather, through particular biblical images, he talked concretely about what enslaved him as a black man and what he hoped for his children in the middle of the twentieth century in the United States of America. Drawing on biblical images and metaphors, King invited his hearers to provide their own concrete examples of oppression and hope.

We need to give our own children no less. A swimming buddy of mine boasts that she will let her children choose their own religion. I bury my shock in the bath towel, wondering on what basis will her children choose? How will they learn a rich language for hope, for despair, for fidelity? There are lots of dialects out there, not all of them articulate or truthful. Rather than the freedom to choose their own religious faith practices, we must teach our children a first language of faith. If they do not already have a language for religious experience, they will have trouble identifying it.

## Doing Something *to* Us

"I stopped going to church because it just wasn't doing anything for me anymore." The complaint is common. People in a consumer culture expect a return on every investment. They expect their cars to run, their employees to work, and their children to be grateful. Even time is a commodity, to be "spent" or "saved" like money. In this universe of values, Christian practices describe a world made strange. Dismantling consumerist mentality practices does something *for* us by doing something *to* us. More precisely, these disciplines of discipleship shape all of our relationships, instruct our emotions, link us to a past and a future, and refocus our vision.

### Shaping Our Relationships

Religious practices describe a relationship to the sacred. As a religion Christianity is not primarily about assenting to doctrine or obeying a code, though these certainly figure. Christianity is primarily about being in relationship with the God revealed in Jesus Christ. The life of discipleship flows out of this relationship with the crucified and risen Christ.

Fourth-century North African theologian Saint Augustine was the quintessential "seeker," and he sought Truth by trying to relate himself to beauty, rhetoric, philosophy, women, and a variety of religions. Conversion to Christianity inspired Augustine to write his spiritual autobiography, *The Confessions*, in which Augustine chronicles his discovery of a central insight about Christianity: Christianity is all about relationship. Surveying the twists and turns of a rich life, he discovered that at the very moments when he had been seeking to fasten himself to Truth, he had already been found by a God who had been with him all along. He sought a "What" and was found by "Someone."

This relationship to Someone shapes all our other relationships. Loving God is like the love of a good marriage, which binds two people together and never seems to run dry. Love operates on a principle of surplus, not one of scarcity. The more love is tapped, the greater the supply, and it touches everything around it. Indeed, the nature of love is to spill over into all other relationships. As the Jews did before him, Jesus drew on love's quality of abundance in his Great Commandment: "You shall love the Lord with all your heart and soul and mind and strength, and you shall love your neighbor as yourself" (Matthew 22:38–39; compare Deuteronomy 6:5). The command describes three edges of a triangle: God, self, and neighbor.

Each edge is crucial. If the relationship to *God* is left out, practices become mere group activities, like a car wash, a bake sale, or some civic group activity. Practices lose their connection with the holy or create it in human form. If the relationship to *self* is erased, practices become the tools of self-erasure. The individual risks being lost in the community. As many Christian feminists have pointed out, self-sacrifice works only when there is a self to offer freely. If the *neighbor* evaporates, practices become experiments in spiritual introspection. The presence of the neighbor takes spirituality out of the psyche and into the actual world of other people. The neighbor helps us test our spiritual vision, lest that vision grow dim.

Church historian Roberta Bondi discusses this triangle of relationships as she reflects on the daily practice of prayer. As a feminist, she struggled with the Lord's Prayer and naming God as a "Father." However, the hardest part of the prayer turned out to be the word *our*. She found herself betrayed by a close friend and colleague, and she had a hard time recognizing this person as another child of God. The prayer to "Our Father" meant she couldn't think of her colleague only as an adversary. Jane Ann was also her sister in Christ. To ease her anger, she deliberately prayed to "My Father—and the Father of Jane Ann." Repeated over a period of days and weeks, that practice made space for reconciliation that Bondi would not have sought on her own.[5]

### Instructing Our Emotions

Just as sinews connect bone to bone, emotions connect people one to another. They are the connective tissue of human society, and they can build up or tear down. We tend to regard emotions as the raw material of human experience: the heart's knee-jerk reaction to stimuli. But emotions are scripted, and we learn from others which ones to summon in response to a situation. We watch how others respond, judge the impact of their anger or joy, and either imitate the response or choose something different. A Croatian American described his childhood neighborhood in Peoria, Illinois. Along with a cluster of other Croatian American families, his family settled across the alley from the Serbian American immigrants. They had learned their hatreds well, and it defined them. Even in the New World, these immigrants needed to be near their Old World enemies. Of such an upbringing, the man wondered: "Who would we have been without our enemies?"

Because of their powerful potential for good and ill, the emotions beg for direction. Sixth-century Italian abbot Saint Benedict of Nursia understood the need for guidance. As abbot to several monastic communities in his lifetime, Benedict gained his wisdom the hard way. A group of unruly monks once tried to poison him, and he knew the perils of community life, particularly a community of people who did not choose to be together. He also knew that many monks did not freely choose monastic life; the monastery had been chosen for them by parents who could not afford to raise them. Judging from the literature of the period, monastic life drew out both the best and the worst emotions in the brothers.

In his *Rule*, Benedict describes eight periods of common prayer that organized the monks' days, beginning with Matins at 2 A.M. and ending with Compline as darkness fell. He devotes a large portion of his *Rule* to these periods of common prayer, outlining with precision which psalms should be said at which time of day. The monks would move through all 150 psalms within the space of a week. Benedict felt this journey through the psalter would direct and instruct the monks' emotions.

How would chanting the psalms instruct the monks' emotional lives? Poet Kathleen Norris describes how they worked on her. She spent time in a Benedictine community, living in the world of the psalms and following St. Benedict's *Rule*: "Quite simply, the Rule spoke to me. Benedict's language and imagery come from the Bible, but he was someone who read the psalms every day—as Benedictines still do—and something of the psalms' emotional honesty, their grounding in the physical, rubbed off on him. Even when the psalms are at their most ecstatic, they convey holiness not with abstraction but with images from the world we know: rivers clap their hands, hills dance like yearling sheep."[6]

The psalms display a broad range of emotions in relationship to God: rejoicing and despair, consolation and abandonment, judgment and mercy. As the brothers chanted them, they could surface these feelings and point them toward God for direction.

## Linking Us to a Past and a Future

Every year I teach a required course on the history of the early church. About the fourth week of the semester, we discuss the ancient Christian creeds: Where did they come from? What were they used for? How do they function today? One year I had a student from a tradition that does not use creeds in its worship, and she posed a question to classmates who used them regularly: "What does saying a creed do to you?" I watched as her classmates struggled to imagine worship without these set pieces of the liturgy. They fumbled for the "right" explanations, then fell silent. The whole truth resisted language. Only part of it could be put into words. The rest was embedded in a lifetime of practice.

Not all Christians recite creeds, but for many this remains an important practice. Creeds rehearse the basics of belief in a way that invites participation rather than offers some pious explanation. I think this is why the students had such a hard time putting into words what it was like to be in a community that uses creeds. Spoken with voices rising and falling in unison, a creed rolls out a sacred story in timeless words of praise and wonder. This is who God is; this is what God has done. To understand what happens, you have to be there. As Christians recite the creeds, they reenter the world the creed opens up.

Christians have spoken these words for centuries; they will continue to be spoken in awe and reverence for centuries to come. In saying the creed, believers take what children's author Madeleine L'Engle calls "a wrinkle in time." The practice invites into the present moment a whole host of witnesses who have spoken the same creed in countless languages across the centuries and around the world. Moreover, the practice anticipates the witness of generations of Christians to come. As these voices past and future swell the chorus, time breaks open and crowds into the present moment.

In such moments, practices reach into the past. That past has solidity and shape; it provides a foundation to build on. Christians do not need to walk into Holy Week or the Christmas season wondering, "What shall we do this year?" The services follow a flexible pattern that believers have observed for centuries. Reenacting the rites of these foremothers and forefathers in the faith, Christians join them across time and space.

Practices also anticipate a future. In engaging in activities that have defined what it means to be a believer for centuries, Christians hand them on by example to generations to come. For example, children learn the practice of prayer through table grace. Invited to add their own thanksgiving, they offer contributions that inform and even delight the rest of the table: "I am grateful that Mom hasn't looked in my room yet." Or "God bless all chocolate cows." A child accustomed to being grateful lives in a world filled with gifts. Gratitude functions like a magnet. A grateful person finds things for which to be thankful. Perhaps the parable of the talents refers to the thankful person and his habit of gratitude in its conclusion: "For to all those who have, more will be given, and they will have an abundance; but from those who have nothing, even what they have will be taken away" (Matthew 25:29). The grateful person anticipates a world of abundance; he feels that everything is gift. He sees himself blessed with whatever he has. In contrast, scarcity, envy, and jealousy are the constant companions of someone who is ungrateful. He never feels he has what he deserves. Everything and everyone remind him that he has less, and the ungrateful person anticipates a world of scarcity. Practicing envy builds toward a different future than practicing gratitude.

## Refocusing Our Vision

Christian practices shape us in peculiar ways, and in the shaping we gain a distinctive angle of vision, a God's-eye view. From this point of view we gain a fresh perspective on the world around us. We pay attention to it in new ways. Moreover, this God's-eye view invites us not only to *see* the world in new ways but to *reimagine* it, to see it as a world created and sustained by the beneficent God. What is the difference that seeing a world according to God might make?

As novelist and occasional philosopher Iris Murdoch reminds us, "We can only choose within the world that we see."[7] Should I give money to the man panhandling outside the post office? The question gets asked only if I have seen him. If I am distracted by the next errand or the last conversation, he may not even enter my field of vision. In a culture dedicated to distraction, attending to what is in front of us presents a real challenge. Cell phones go off in the middle of a symphony or a lecture; TV provides background noise in too many households, a substitute for conversation. Headsets, video games, digital watches beeping the hour—is it any wonder we have trouble focusing on what is in front of us?

Distraction is not only a problem for twenty-first-century Christians. The biblical record reveals that the disciples of Jesus had similar trouble focusing. They consistently tried to steer their master away from what was in front of him: a blind beggar, a crowd of rowdy children, a Samaritan woman. In their eyes, Jesus had more important people to speak with and more pressing matters demanding his attention.

Yet Jesus consistently breaks free of their agenda anxiety to pay attention. He heals the blind man; he blesses the children; he speaks to the stranger. Ignoring the disciples' plans for his future, Jesus attends to what is in front of him. He is fully present to whoever crosses his path. This kind of attention stands as both a rebuke and a plea to the myopic disciples: "Look at what's in front of you, and pay attention! What could be more important than this!"

Imagination plays an important role in seeing the world according to God. This capacity employs creativity and attention to see what is and understand it as part of a larger whole. The homeless person panhandling outside the post office could be seen as the sum of his deficits. After all, he is without money, without a home, without a family, without a job. This way of looking at him suggests a certain course of action. Having seen the man as homeless, jobless, and friendless, I would scurry past without meeting his gaze. I could also image this man as a child of God, an interpretation that suggests very different responses. I could meet his gaze and smile. I could give him some food or money. I could tell him where he could find shelter for the night. How a passerby treats a panhandler depends largely on how she sees him, not simply through the eyes of sight, but also through the eyes of mind and heart.

Faith practices train the vision of the mind and heart. They function as the eye exercises of the soul; they help disciples see better. Anyone who enters the world of the psalms, as Benedict's monks did, could not fail to notice the poor: "Who is like the Lord our God? He raises the poor from the dust, and lifts the needy from the ash heap" (Psalms 113:5–7). Those who worship this kind of God follow suit, and gradually they gain a God's-eye view of things. The Holiness Code of Leviticus gives another reason for such concern. At the heart of its message is "the widow, the orphan, the stranger in your land." Why is this? The writer is adamant: "For you were strangers in the land of Egypt: I am the Lord your God" (Leviticus 19:33–34). God did not abandon the Israelites to slavery in Egypt, and they were exhorted to show similar compassion to the strangers in their midst. Such scriptural texts read in prayer and chanted in worship shape the heart and tutor the imagination.

Imagining the world according to God affects not only how we see others but how we see ourselves. Bringing imagination into an encounter with a panhandler changes how I imagine myself. Recalling the parable of the Good Samaritan, I refrain from cataloguing everyone as "neighbor" or "non-neighbor." Instead, I take the parable's counsel and think of how I might best be a "neighbor" to this man in front of me. The view of both the panhandler and myself alters.

This seems like a lot to think about in front of the post office. Or is it? The world of a disciple certainly looks different from the world of someone who had never set foot in the biblical terrain of parable and psalm. The God-shaped imagination asks two questions: "How shall I interpret what I have seen?" and "How can I be a neighbor?"

## Reframing a World According to God

This book argues that the core practices of the Christian faith *reframe* some of the most intransigent moral issues we face in today's world. The metaphor of framing is important. We frame something we want to look at: a picture, a photograph, an oil painting. A frame contains it, allows focus, showcases some parts and blocks out others. Often we frame with our hands something we want to look at in a landscape, focusing and blotting out blinding sunlight or a messy tangle of telephone lines. Another person, looking at the same landscape, might frame the telephone lines instead. Still another would simply find a frame large enough to capture it all.

A similar kind of framing happens when we consider an ethical issue. How we describe a situation determines its outcome. Take a familiar illustration. In its television commercials, Archer Daniels Midland presents itself as "supermarket to the world." This is how the company wants to be seen in a global economy. The moral issue lies in how the company sees the world. "Supermarket to the world" assumes a world of consumers and shoppers, buyers and sellers, a kind of global Great Mall. Only in such a world would a supermarket make any kind of sense. But is the world really like this? This point of view obscures all the people who cannot afford to shop. They never enter the picture at all: they are literally outside the frame of this picture. They become invisible.

The practices of discipleship frame a world according to God. They accompany disciples along a journey that begins in baptism and ends in resurrection. Baptism inaugurates the journey; the

Lord's Supper provides food and drink; prayer connects us to the One whom we follow; forgiveness allows us to go forward together; remembering the dead offers us the counsel of the saints who have gone before; and fidelity makes community possible in the first place. Let us begin the journey.

# 2

. . . . . . . . . . . . . . . . . . . . . . . . . . . . . . . .

# Discipleship

## Meeting Peter Again for the First Time

In the midst of a locker room discussion of religion, a woman asked me, "Are you a practicing Christian?" The word *practicing* caught my attention, "No, I got it right the first time," I said, and we both laughed. In fact, I need all the practice I can get. As I reflected more on the exchange, I realized how little in fact I had "gotten it right" and how much discipleship had gotten me, placing me in a community of people who, like myself, need all the practice they can get. That exercise is graciously provided in a series of God-shaped and God-shaping practices that sustain us on the journey of discipleship.

We are also sustained by a company of disciples who extend throughout the centuries and around the world. Before examining more closely some of the core practices Jesus left behind, I want to draw on the wisdom of that first company of disciples, particularly Peter. We contemporary disciples take our bearings from these first followers of Jesus. As we study the rough map they left for us in the biblical record, we discover several dimensions of discipleship. Discipleship is first and foremost the journey into a relationship that deepens and grows. The first disciples left their fishing nets to follow Jesus of Nazareth; after the resurrection, they shifted their loyalty to the risen Christ. The relationship began with a call, and that call orients disciples then and now: "Follow me." Along the journey, no disciple travels alone. Christian discipleship is inherently social, and practices sustain the community the disciples have formed among themselves and with others. As we examine each of these dimensions of discipleship, we ask Peter to be our guide. His story is also our own.

## Discipleship: A Journey into Relationship

If someone says she is a disciple, I immediately want to know "of whom?" or "of what?" If someone says, "I'm a disciple of Aum Shin Rikyo" or "Osama bin Laden," I head for the exit. If someone says, "I'm a disciple of globalization," I settle in for a long conversation. If someone says, "I'm a disciple of the blues," I gain valuable information about the person's musical tastes. Discipleship demands an object of one's loyalty, and in that demand it is a lot like love. When someone declares "I love . . . ," we wait for the sentence to be completed. We want to know the object of this affection. Discipleship, like love, describes a relationship, and that relationship requires a follower and someone or something worth following.

Christian discipleship goes even farther. The relationship described in Christian discipleship is a relationship with a person, not a belief system or even a righteous cause. Disciples relate to some One, not some Thing. Early in his ministry, Jesus asked his disciples a question that underscores the personal dimension of Christian discipleship: "Who do you say that I am?" (Mark 8:29; Matthew 16:15; Luke 9:20). The way Jesus posed the question was crucial. He did not ask, "What do you understand by religion?" or "What do you believe?" He did not even ask, "Who do you think God is?" Jesus' question was different: "Who do you say that I am?"

Jesus poses the question to disciples today, and he is looking for a certain kind of answer, an answer that is concrete and particular. He is not interested in an abstract theological discussion; he does not want the theologian's answer or the pastor's answer. He asks only for the answer *I* would give, because, after all, Jesus is in relationship with *me*. For example, if my husband asks, "Do you love me?" and I rush off to consult *Bartlett's Familiar Quotations* or respond with a lengthy discourse on love, I am not going to come up with the right answer. My partner wants the answer that comes from the heart, more specifically, the answer that comes from *my* heart.

In posing the question to Peter, "Who do you say that I am?" Jesus sought Peter's heart's response. And Peter gave it. Mark's Gospel records Peter's answer: "You are the Messiah!" Good Jews like Peter understood that the Messiah would come as a liberator, an anointed ruler who would end Roman occupation and restore the royal throne of David. In calling Jesus "Messiah," Peter cast him as the Strong Warrior in a great military drama. No doubt Peter also cast himself as first officer in the Messiah's army of liberation, but Jesus quickly dispelled his illusions by speaking of himself as the "Son of Man" who would undergo great suffering. Peter was shocked, and he took Jesus aside and tried to silence him. Jesus resisted, rebuking Peter as "Satan! Get behind me" (Mark 8:27–33). Peter answered from the heart, and he made the wrong answer. Yet Peter's answer did not end the relationship. Peter continued to follow, and Jesus continued to lead. The bond of loyalty between the two, disciple and master, survived mistaken identity.

Christian discipleship describes a kind of mutual bonding between the one who follows and the one who is followed. Discipleship expresses our loyalty to Jesus but also his loyalty to us. This mutuality is unusual. Some gurus demand loyalty from their devotees but do not always offer it in return. A guru would probably have dismissed Peter as an unworthy and clueless follower. With Christian discipleship, the situation is different. Jesus' loyalty to his disciples exceeded the loyalty he received in return. At this point in the journey, Peter did not yet understand who Jesus was. His own fantasies and needs blinded him. This could have been grounds for dismissal, but Jesus did not abandon Peter. Instead, he tried again. Mark's Gospel offers a clue to interpreting this rough exchange between Jesus and Peter. Immediately preceding it, the group encountered a blind man who wanted to see (Mark 8:22–26). Jesus put spit on the man's eyes and asked him what he saw. The man responded, "I can see people, but they look like trees, walking" (8:24). Jesus could have walked away, chalking the encounter up to a failed miracle. But Jesus tried again. A second time he placed his hand on the blind man's eyes. This time the man's eyes were opened.

This healing story interprets the exchange between Jesus and Peter. Like the blind man, Peter has bad vision. His confession "You are the Messiah!" translates as "I see you, but you look like the Strong Warrior from the desert!" Trees don't walk, any more than Jesus qualified as some Strong Warrior who would defeat Roman rule. As he did with the blind man, Jesus tried again. He rebuked Peter, but he did not desert him: "Get behind me!" is not the same as "Get out of my life!" The journey continued, and Peter was still on it.

Friendship and frustration, affection and sheer cluelessness: all find their place within the mutual love of discipleship. Discipleship means that Jesus tries again with us. His love for the disciples far exceeds their love for him. Jesus loves the disciples into loving him more fully. As their love deepens, the disciples change.

The question Jesus poses to Peter and to each of us serves another purpose. Our answer tells him who we think *he* is; it also tells him who we think *we* are. How we answer the question "Who do you say that I am?" tells us who we are. What we love shapes us. Purveyors of good food would have us believe that we are what we eat, but we are shaped more deeply by what we love. As Saint Augustine put it, our loves (*amores*) form our habits (*mores*). Our loves shape who we are and how we are in the world. Parents of teenagers worry quite concretely about love's power to shape identity and action: "You are the company you keep!" Parents fret about the company their children keep because they know the power of love to form or malform people, to shape or misshape them.

In asking his disciples "Who do you say that I am?" Jesus found out how the disciples saw themselves. When they saw in Jesus a

Strong Warrior, they imagined themselves to be desert revolution-aries, shock troops in Yahweh's Foreign Legion. When they saw in Jesus one of the prophets, they imagined themselves to be heralds of the return of prophecy to Israel. When they saw Jesus as Elijah, they imagined that they could hold on to his robes and be caught up into the heavens. But Jesus was none of these figures, and the disciples' identity had to change accordingly.

Jesus taught his disciples that the Son of Man must be perse-cuted, suffer, die, and on the third day rise again. The disciples had not seen Jesus as the suffering Son of Man because they did not want to imagine themselves following that kind of a leader. But Jesus was the company they kept; if the suffering Son of Man was his story, it would be theirs as well.

"Who do you say that I am?" The question was important for disciples then, and it is important for disciples now. When we call on the name of Jesus, whom do we address? I use Jesus' question to organize my introductory course in early church history because it helps sort out the various responses of the earliest Christian com-munities. I also ask my students to think about how they would answer, and we discuss our various responses. One day early in the semester after discussing our images of Jesus, I walked into class and my students were busy drawing their pictures of Jesus with crayons on butcher paper that had been scattered around the classroom. After everyone had finished, we presented our images. The pictures displayed the many faces of Jesus as well as the many faiths of my students.

## Inviting Us to Be Disciples

In this new millennium, there are a lot of people looking for spiritual masters. These would-be disciples cast about for the perfect guru and search out the most effective spiritual fix. A sense of spiritual dislocation motivates some. Dissatisfaction with the churches of their childhood spurs others on. All of these potential disciples assume that they can choose the perfect master the same way one chooses a laundry detergent. They all assume they can summon up the perfect spiritual path the way one manipulates icons on a computer screen.

Ironically, Christian discipleship is not a matter of *choosing* but rather of *being chosen*. Christian discipleship is not so much a matter of seeking as one of being found. Words from the hymn "Amazing Grace" state this insight well: "I once was lost, but now am found,/Was blind, but now I see." Disciples of Christ are "found" by being called. In a consumer culture, the notion of calling seems outdated. Consumers are more familiar with choosing than being chosen, and they choose everything from their breakfast cereal to their spiritual path. Spirituality seems to be a product like any other commodity. If it fails to meet expectations, choose something that yields a better return. If it does not live up to certain expectations, there is probably something more stylish out there. If someone else has something that works better, get one like theirs.

Is consumerism the right model for spirituality? In an interview on National Public Radio, historian of religions Huston Smith relates an encounter with a holy man in India. The guru had watched would-be disciples come and go like the seasons, and he wondered how long his teachings had stuck with them. With some amusement he commented on the tendency to choose spiritual paths as one would choose an outfit or a living room set. "If you want to reach water," he asked, "why would you want to drill twelve wells only five feet deep? Why not drill one well sixty feet deep? Then you just might hit water."

Christian discipleship is not like shopping. In their former lives, the disciples who were part of Jesus' original group of twelve were not shopping for a master. They fished; they collected taxes; they had families. One of the disciples, Nathanael, was probably a rabbi. In John's Gospel, we first meet him sitting under a fig tree (1:48), a shady place he could have used as an impromptu classroom. Unlike the teachers and rabbis around him, however, Jesus did not stay in one place so that people could find him. Jesus did not wait to be found. In all the biblical accounts, Jesus was the one in motion. He sought and found his disciples over and over again. The words he used were always the same: "Follow me." Throughout the journey, Jesus repeated the call. The only words he said more frequently to the disciples were the words "Be not afraid."

This was no coincidence. The two commands go together. If we follow Jesus, we will be taken places we would not have chosen otherwise. We will be in situations over which we have no control. We will be drawn outside the prison of our desires. Again, it is Peter who shows us the character of discipleship. In a postresurrection appearance recorded at the end of John's Gospel, Jesus said to Peter, "When you were younger, you used to fasten your own belt and to go wherever you wished. But when you grow old, you will stretch out your hands, and someone else will fasten a belt around you and take you where you do not wish to go." Jesus concluded this disturbing prophecy with the words "Follow me" (John 21:19).

The words are haunting, but they point to a fundamental difference between disciples and would-be disciples. Would-be disciples, like shoppers, operate under the illusion of control. They think they know what they want. For disciples, being on the journey transforms desire. We know we are not in control. We want only to follow Jesus. Again, Peter gives voice to this desire. When many in the crowd had deserted him, Jesus asked his disciples if they wanted to desert him too. Peter answered, "Lord, to whom can we go? You have the words of eternal life" (John 6:68). Someone else was in control, and that knowledge brought a certain measure of relief. For all the times the disciples faltered in their steps, Jesus offered reassurance: "Be not afraid."

Two commands sustain the journey of discipleship: "Follow me" and "Be not afraid." Another incident with Peter brings them together. Matthew's Gospel records an incident near the Sea of Galilee, where Jesus had been with crowds day and night. He escaped with his disciples in a boat, pushing off to the other side of the lake. When they reached the far shore, Jesus left the disciples in the boat and went ashore to find a quiet place to pray. Darkness fell, and a storm blew in. Borne by wind-tossed waves, the boat drifted away from the shore. The disciples fought to return to the shore, and Jesus came to them instead, walking on the water back toward the boat. The disciples did not recognize Jesus: they thought they were seeing a ghost. Jesus called out to them: "Take heart, it is I; do not be afraid" (Matthew 14:27).

Peter wanted to walk on the water just like Jesus. This time, though, he had learned something. He knew that he could not come until he was called, and he asked Jesus to call him: "Command me to come to you on the water" (Matthew 14:28). Jesus obliged: "Come." The wind was high; the waves were ragged; Peter's enthusiasm quickly turned to fear. Once again Jesus stuck with this disciple, offering him a hand and safe passage back to the boat.

Many commentators see in this passage a negative example of the steady faith disciples ought to exhibit. As Peter's faith faltered, he sank. Viewed from the perspective of discipleship, however, the passage underscores a true and inescapable dimension of calling. This time Peter got it right. Before venturing anywhere, Peter knew that he needed to be called. He asked Jesus to call him.

Peter's story makes something else clear. As he did with Peter, Jesus calls us over and over again, if only we can stop to listen. Jesus called Peter both when Peter asked to be called and when he did not. Indeed, the first and the last words Jesus spoke to Peter were the words "Follow me." The command frames the life of discipleship. At the beginning of his ministry, Jesus called Peter, urging him away from his nets. Then, at the end of his ministry and before his ascent into heaven, the risen Christ left Peter with the command. John's Gospel records Jesus' final conversation with Peter (John 21:15 ff.). He asked Peter three times: "Do you love me?" We sense Peter's mounting exasperation, but it was as if each profession of love erased one of Peter's three denials of Jesus in the night in which he was betrayed. Jesus gave Peter a second chance to rebuild the relationship of discipleship from the ground up: "Yes, Lord, you know that I love you."

Then Jesus responded with a gripping portrait of old age: "When you grow old, you will stretch out your hands, and someone else will fasten a belt around you and take you where you do not wish to go" (John 21:18). Those who have cared for an elderly friend or relative know the gesture well. Peter may have recognized it himself, because by all accounts, he himself had a mother-in-law so infirm that Jesus was called in to heal her (Matthew 8:14–17; Mark 1:29–34; Luke 4:38–41). Perhaps Jesus' image recalled to him that miraculous healing; perhaps Peter thought about his nearly fatal attempt to walk on water. Perhaps he remembered an exchange that now embarrassed him, when he had declared Jesus the Messiah, the Strong Warrior from the desert. In that instant, Peter wanted to fasten his own belt around his waist and gird himself with sword and shield for battle against the Romans. Instead, Jesus had taken him where he did not wish to go, following a suffering Son of Man. Perhaps Jesus' image took Peter back to their first encounter, as he and his brother Andrew flung their nets into the sea. Jesus had said to him then what he said now: "Follow me."

What a journey it had been! What a tough traveling companion Peter turned out to be. He was either overly enthusiastic, excitedly offering to build booths for Moses and Elijah on the Mount of Olives, or he appeared overly tired, barely able to keep watch while Jesus prayed. The real joke of the Gospel accounts was that Jesus called Peter "Cephas," or "Rocky." The title initially seemed like a compliment. Now maybe even Peter suspected it referred more to his thick skull and general confusion. Nonetheless, Jesus kept calling Peter. And if he continued to call Peter, he will surely continue to call us.

## A Journey into Community

Discipleship is also a journey into community, both the community among the disciples and the community in which they serve. Following Jesus, disciples learn how to interact with one another and how to interface with the world. As Peter's story makes clear, disciples did not choose Jesus—he chose them. There was no accounting for Jesus' taste, at least no human way of accounting for it. Jesus chose fishermen and scholars, tax collectors and revolutionaries. Moreover, Jesus showed compassion recklessly, not just to the disciples, but to those in the larger company of people who followed him. The disciples themselves could never predict who would fall within the embrace of this man's mercy. Just when it seemed that Jesus was going to come out against the Jews, he praised the faith of one of the high priests. Just when it seemed that Jesus was going to censure the Romans, he healed the son of a centurion. Just when it seemed Jesus would rage against the wealthy, he headed for the home of his rich friends, Martha, Mary, and Lazarus. Women were part of Jesus' entourage—and they were strong women. In Jesus' company there were immigrants, both legal and illegal, mixed-race folk, Gentiles, Samaritans, Syro-Phoenicians, even children. And children were about as invisible a group in the ancient world as there could be. How often the crowd of people closest to Jesus found themselves wishing that he had just stuck with fishermen or Jews or women or men! It would certainly have made the journey easier to bear. Jesus seemed to have very eclectic tastes.

The differences among the community of disciples was not a recipe for easy community life. The only thing most of Jesus' followers had in common was Jesus himself—and perhaps their confusion over his puzzling ways. The disciples did not always get along. Like the Israelites in the desert, they murmured among themselves, against each other and against Jesus. They competed with one another over who will be greatest or smartest, and the mother of James and John constantly schemed to get her sons places of privilege in this world or the next. The disciples accused each other of treachery or stealing. John's Gospel always parenthetically reminds the reader that Judas kept the common purse. The disciples closest to Jesus tried to insulate him from all the "wrong people": women, children, blind beggars, Pharisees, Romans,

Syro-Phoenicians, or Samaritans. They were convinced that certain classes or ethnicities, genders or occupations, physical abilities or disabilities disqualified people from Jesus' presence. Subverting all attempts at control, Jesus included whomever he wanted in his company of followers.

The disciples scattered when Jesus needed them most, leaving him to be crucified between two common thieves, not two of his disciples. The disciples were not even around to be convicted. The disciples made up a rowdy lot, edgy and hard to get along with. There is no evidence, however, that Jesus regretted choosing a single one of them. He lived among them; he endured their infighting; he refused to let them cramp his style; and he loved them with abandon. Jesus continued to associate with the most unlikely people, and he urged his disciples to do the same: "Go and do likewise." That mandate displays a second dimension of community: the communities into which the disciples are drawn.

Jesus traveled with an eclectic company of people. That fact received much comment. All of the Gospels record a common judgment: "Look, a glutton and a drunkard, a friend of tax collectors and sinners!" (Luke 7:34). In the eyes of many, Jesus ate and drank with all the wrong kinds of people. Yet the jeers of his enemies revealed a powerful truth about Jesus' community. In the world of the ancient Near East, friendship meant table fellowship. People ate and drank with friends. According to this ancient etiquette, the people with whom one shares one's table were friends.

Jesus modeled a kind of friendship that goes beyond charity. Charity dictates giving money to the poor, giving food to the hungry, and giving drink to the thirsty. Often the one giving remains anonymous and invisible to the one receiving. Jesus dared to be known. Instead of giving money, Jesus walked with the poor; instead of giving food, he ate with them; instead of giving water or wine, he drank with them. He invited people to know him. Jesus dared to dine with, drink with, and be at table with people who were considered worthless and treated as invisible.

Jesus willfully disregarded the "no trespassing" signs of his time. To understand how outrageous this must have seemed, remember what it was like in the early 1960s for African Americans in the Deep South to attempt to sit at the front of the bus or eat at a white lunch counter. Jesus is like the white man in the Civil Rights Era South who gives up his seat on a bus so that an older black woman can sit down. Jesus is like a black girl who endures taunts to attend a desegregated school. No wonder Jesus' behavior got attention! He brought together people who would never have encountered each other otherwise.

Jesus told his disciples, "Go and do likewise" (Luke 10:37). That command concluded a parable he told in response to a lawyer's question: "And who is my neighbor?" (10:29). In the story of the Good Samaritan, Jesus refused to indulge in the lawyer's game of cataloguing people as "neighbors," "not neighbors," and "occasional neighbors." Instead, he presented a parable that pressed the lawyer to examine whether he acted as a neighbor or not. The parable presents an unlikely hero. Jews despised Samaritans and could recite a whole history of reasons to justify their rage. The latest offense would have been fresh in the minds of Luke's readers. Within their lifetime, Samaritans had scattered bones of a corpse in the Temple at Jerusalem during Passover, an act that defiled the sacred space and closed it down for the annual ceremonies accompanying those holy days. Jesus' audience would have had a hard time seeing a Samaritan cast in the role of hero. Everyone regarded Samaritans as demons.

In the parable Jesus told, a man was stripped, robbed, and left for dead. Both a priest and a Levite passed by without stopping. Perhaps they suspected that the man was dead or almost dead. They wanted to avoid contact with a corpse, which violated Jewish law and defiled them. Perhaps they wondered if the man was a countryman, friend or foe. Clothes would have identified him for them, but the man was naked, stripped of all identification. We do not know the motivation of these pious men, and apparently it did not matter. What mattered was that they passed by a dying man. In a story full of identification tags (a Levite, a Samaritan, a priest), the reader never finds out who this man is or where he came from. He remains unmarked and unidentified, open to whatever anyone wants to think of him. The Samaritan alone stopped, saw the man, and attended to him.

The hearers of this parable never knew why the Samaritan stopped to attend to the beaten man. But Jesus makes it clear that those who follow him will see things differently. After following Jesus for a time, disciples begin to see the world as he does. They begin to notice the poor because he does. They watch out for children because he blesses them. They hear a blind man bellowing outside the gates of Jericho. They ask themselves why a woman would come to draw water from the town well in the heat of the day when she would be unlikely to encounter anyone else. Following Jesus, the disciples begin to see the world that he sees. It is a world according to God.

## Seeing a World According to God

"Follow me." Jesus repeats these words again and again throughout the Gospels. The ragged crew of disciples apparently needed the repetition, because at times Jesus sounded like a broken record. These are important words to all those who would follow Jesus today. Being a Christian is not about following rules or doctrines. It is first and last about following Jesus; it is about being in relationship with the living God. In the person of Jesus Christ, God walked on earth; through the presence of the Spirit, God hovers still over the whole of creation.

The question every disciple wants to know is this: "Where do we find Jesus today?" A group of core practices help disciples locate the body of Christ in the world. They are not the only places where Christ is present, but by engaging in them, we learn to recognize Christ when he is present. These activities, elaborated in scripture and done in the name of the living God, make Christ present.

This book examines these corporate activities as practices of discipleship: baptism, the Lord's Supper, prayer, forgiveness, remembering the dead, and fidelity. These are places where God has promised to be present. Some churches call some of these corporate actions sacraments; others call them gifts. Others just do them, without bothering to catalogue them. The point is that all Christians do them. These actions define who they are; they describe a world according to God.

Faith practices find their roots in the life of Jesus and their place in the world. For those wishing to become a part of the way of life called "Christian," faith practices describe the way of life that constitutes discipleship. They are the disciplines of discipleship. We may at times do them by rote or routine, but they orient us on the journey of discipleship. We do not make the journey alone: we travel with a whole company of disciples from around the world and across the centuries. We do not make the journey without a map: practices orient us to the One whom we follow. In John's Gospel, Jesus promises to send the Holy Spirit, the Comforter: he will not leave them without comfort (John 14:18). Nor does Jesus leave them without compass. As they have for centuries, practices point disciples to the person they love and display the path they follow. Like the polestar, they point disciples to the direction of the true north.

# 3

. . . . . . . . . . . . . . . . . . . . . . . . . . . . . . . . .

# Baptism

## *Joining the Journey*

Anyone who travels in Italy learns to watch hands. They do so much; they tell you everything. If you don't speak Italian, you have to watch hands even more carefully, gauging each gesture for clues. Should you go here or there? Are you being welcomed or dismissed? Should you be cautious or quick?

I remember watching a man using a pay phone step outside the phone booth because there was no room for him to gesture inside. Although none of his gestures could be seen by the person on the other end of the line, he could not manage to speak without his hands. I eavesdropped on an entire conversation an old woman was having without understanding a word. I simply watched her hands. They fluttered like birds, punctuating every sentence.

Hands are part of the world according to God, both God's history with us and our history with God. Divine handprints are all over the Old Testament. Hands lift Moses out of the bulrushes. Hands release a raven, then a dove across storm-tossed waters. Hands reach across the Red Sea to part mighty waves. Hands push their way into the Levitical codes to define the times when a husband could or could not touch his wife. Hands crowd the psalms of David: angry hands knotted into fists and shaken at God in lamentation, happy hands shaking timbrels in joy. The psalmist points to the hands of God endlessly creating: "When I look at your heavens, the work of your fingers" (Psalms 8:3). In the face of injustice, the psalmist pleads for God to "lift up your hand" to stay attacks against the widow, the orphan, the strangers in the land (Psalms 10:12).

Hands figure prominently in the Gospels as well. We cannot help but notice Jesus' hands as he takes dirt, makes a paste of it, and smears it on the eyelids of a blind man. He "stretched out his hand and touched" a leper (Matthew 8:3; Mark 1:41; Luke 5:13). Indeed, Jesus touches all the "untouchable" people of his time: the dead, the defiled, the lepers. Jesus' ministry could be summed up as a story of hands. Is it any wonder that Mary Magdalene reaches out to touch her risen Lord? Or that Thomas remains in doubt until he can place his fingers in Jesus' side? Both of these disciples seek hands-on confirmation that their Lord is alive. In both the Old and New Testaments, hands narrate the world according to God.

Hands speak eloquently of God's history with us; they also narrate our history with God. That history begins at the baptismal font, where hands work powerfully to lift up new Christians, bring them into a new family, and cradle them in a new identity. Whatever baptism's denominational choreography, hands perform the promises that baptism speaks. Hands present the candidate to the pastor or priest, who takes the new Christian in hand. Hands submerge the candidate into water, plunging her into the waters of life, death, and resurrection. Hands lift the newly baptized up out of the water and into the midst of the assembly so that all may see and welcome this new brother or sister in Christ. If the new Christian is an adult, hands thrust her forward into a new family. Dipped in scented holy oil, hands trace the sign of the cross on this new Christian's forehead. In some ceremonies, hands draw the baptized near, as the pastor or priest whispers in her ear an ancient Aramaic word of exorcism, "Ephphatha!" (Mark 7:34). Finally, hands hold the Paschal candle as the new Christian receives the light of Christ. Not only God's history with us but also our history with God begins with hands.

The hands-on ceremony of baptism claims us as Christians and names us as "Children of God." Christians are children who joyfully acknowledge their origins, and baptism bonds them to a Father in heaven, a Brother who died and rose from the dead, and a new family of brothers and sisters in Christ. As Christians grow into these new relationships, the ceremony of baptism become a practice. What begins at the font becomes a way of life.

It may seem odd to think of baptism as a practice or a way of life. Most Christians regard baptism as a one-time-only event, and we celebrate baptisms the way we celebrate births. You're born once; you get baptized once. Baptism lies somewhere in the distant past. It is over and done with; it has been taken care of. God's truth, however, is that baptism takes care of us throughout the life of discipleship. For traditions that understand baptism as a sacrament, it is a daily sacrament. For traditions that view it as a rite of initiation, it is an open-ended event. Whether chosen *by* the believer (believer's baptism) or chosen *for* the believer (infant baptism), baptism is ongoing, because Christians return to baptism to hear words that were spoken there and to deepen relationships that were established there. Both the words and the relationships sustain us on the journey of discipleship.

Baptism is both a ceremony and a practice. As a ceremony, baptism initiates the journey of discipleship, welcoming Christians to join in. As a practice, however, baptism offers a map for the road ahead. In addition, baptism introduces us to people who will accompany us along the way. We meet Jesus our Brother as we receive the same identity he did, "Child of God." We encounter God as the one whom Jesus called "Father," which welcomes us into a whole new relationship with the divine. Incorporated into the body of Christ through baptism, we become Jesus' hands in the world. Finally, we gain a whole new family of brothers and sisters in Christ as we reach out to all the children of the world.

## The Cartography of Baptism

I remember trying to do a difficult dive off the three-meter board. My coach had been clear about what to do and when to do it, but there was still a lot to keep track of. I would get to the end of the board and freeze, having forgotten a key piece of what I needed to go forward. By then, of course, I had lost the momentum I needed for the dive ahead. I had to start all over again, circling back to the other end of the board and more instruction from my coach. Each time I had a little more information, a little more encouragement, and a clearer picture of what would happen next. But the only way I was going to get off the board was to start all over again.

The journey of discipleship is a lot like learning to dive. It feels like it runs in circles, and we move forward only by beginning all over again. We return to the call we received in baptism; we move forward only through its promises. The call orients us to the journey of discipleship just like the run down a three-meter board orients a diver to the jackknife ahead. The call baptism issues is the simple invitation: "Follow me." All of the baptismal liturgies, whether simple or elaborate, boil down to this simple invitation to follow.

"Follow me." Jesus beckoned his first disciples with these words, and the invitation was so compelling it did not need elaboration. All of the Gospels agree that at the sound of these words, they dropped everything and followed him. Along the way, however, the disciples faltered and fell out of step. They longed for the lives they had left behind, even the monotony of fishing and the invariant rhythm of tides. They missed friends and family they now saw all too infrequently. Like the Israelites in the desert, they murmured against their leader. They complained to Jesus, whining, "Look, we have left everything and followed you" (Mark 10:28). The evangelist does not record the next line, but it must have been—"and look where that got us." Again and again Jesus reissued the invitation: "Follow me."

As we have seen in Peter's story, Jesus kept his disciples on track by urging them again and again to follow him. Today's disciples return to baptism for the encouragement they need to go forward. Baptism initiates the journey; baptism nudges us forward along the way. Christians advance by returning to the invitation baptism makes: "Follow me." If we are to stay the course of discipleship, we will need to hear these words again and again. Like hikers consulting their compass in unfamiliar territory, disciples return to baptism to take their bearings. We circle back to baptism, certain that we will find Jesus there with the direction we need.

Sometimes, though, we don't even know we need direction. We don't even know we are lost. Several years ago I encountered a small boy standing alone in the cereal aisle at a supermarket with no adult in sight. I went up to the child: "Are you lost?" I asked. He broke away from the enticing array of breakfast possibilities and said, "No. I'm choosing a cereal." The boy did not know where he was; he depended on being found. And he was found, a few minutes later, by a relieved mother who had been searching up and down for him. Like a dependable parent, Jesus sought out his disciples—even when they did not know they were lost. As we have seen with Peter's confession of Jesus as "Messiah, Strong Warrior from the desert," Peter was lost in his own plans for Jesus' ministry, and Jesus circled back to find him. Jesus scolded him, much as the mother must have scolded her young son lost in the cereal aisle. But Jesus did not abandon Peter, and if Jesus hung on to Peter, he will surely hang on to us.

One rainy afternoon in Scotland, my husband and I had just made it back to our lodgings when a Highlands downpour began. Drying our boots in front of the fire, we turned on the television to find that the local Saturday afternoon programming featured contests of sheep-herding dogs, each one competing against the clock to round up an unruly and diffident herd of sheep. There was nothing else on, and we were tired and soggy, so we fell into the drama of herding sheep. As I watched the dogs work the herd, I realized how helpless sheep are. Sheep dither. They wander off; they mill about aimlessly. Without good sheep-herding dogs, sheep would surely be an endangered species. They survive only by dint of a vigilant dog, endlessly circling back and nudging stragglers into the herd. The only way sheep move forward at all is thanks to the tireless teamwork of a shepherd and his dog. I said aloud, "Well, I am the Good Shepherd," and this is exactly what good shepherding involves. Jesus circled back to his own herd of unruly disciples, watching for stragglers and driving them back into the herd. Circling back was the only way the journey of discipleship could go forward.

Peter's story signals to Christians that discipleship always runs in circles, returning again and again to the invitation made in baptism: "Follow me." Disciples have been travelers since Jesus first beckoned a tired fisherman beside the waters of Galilee. In the ancient church, people referred to Jesus' followers as "People of the Way." Christians refused to follow Caesar, a particular family, or a cherished ideology. Christians followed Jesus—wherever he would lead them. In the Middle Ages, this sense of being on a journey combined with a vibrant cult of the saints. Disciples took to highway and byway, journeying to visit the relics of holy men and women: a splinter of the True Cross, a finger of Saint Anne, the site where Saint James was buried.

The practice of pilgrimage made discipleship a journey in fact. But it could be a dangerous journey, costly and even fatal. Though there were hostels along the way where pilgrims could find food and safe lodging, there were also thieves and brigands ready to fleece them, rob them—and worse. Protestant reformers disparaged the practice of pilgrimage, protesting that Christians were reconciled to God by grace through faith and not by pilgrimage. Yet the reformers could not shake the sense that discipleship was a journey, if not to some holy site or relic, then to the holy waters of baptism. Martin Luther made baptism the site of pilgrimage, and it was a pilgrimage open to all Christians and undertaken daily. This journey did not trace a path through rough seas or mountain passes, nor did it lead pilgrims down deserted highways and treacherous alleys. The journey that baptism charted looked more like a circle, as Christians returned again and again to its living waters. Luther counseled a "daily return" to baptism because baptism was the hostel pilgrims sought, a safe haven where Christians would daily be nourished, comforted, and reoriented. He answered in hearty affirmative the prophet's rueful question: "Are we like sheep who have gone astray?" Yes! And daily return to baptism would keep Christians from straying. If they wanted to follow Jesus, no need to don pilgrim's cloak and staff, suit up, and ship for Rome or Santiago de Compostela—no need even to leave the house. A daily return to baptism would give Christians the compass they needed for the journey of discipleship.

The journey might not be an easy one. Like medieval pilgrimages, the journey of discipleship might entail suffering, persecution, and death. Pilgrim's garb marked these travelers as easy prey. In similar ways, baptism turns Christians into marked men and women, making them targets for everything and everyone whom evil holds in its thrall. Yet while baptism makes us more visible, it also gives us the power to stand up to evil. Baptized into the death of Jesus, we rest assured that we are also baptized into his resurrection. The confrontation with powers and principalities will end not at the cross but at the empty tomb. Thus through baptism we enter into a deepening relationship with a new family, with Jesus and his destiny, and with the world.

## Companions Along the Way

I remember attending a baptism that set the stage for a tug-of-war: on one side the claims of blood, and on the other the claims of baptism. Both biological and Christian families struggled for possession of the unsuspecting Mary Charlotte Cadigan, who at six months remained oblivious to it all. Before the service, she rested in the arms of her mother in a white dress of antique lace. "That thing has been in our family for generations," her mother confided to me. "I wore it for my baptism; my mother wore it for hers. Her grandmother and great-grandmother wore it before her." In addition to the sartorial claim the dress made, the family assembled the tribe, inviting hordes of relatives who dutifully appeared in their Sunday best. Invitations to the ceremony featured the child's name in lavish script, which made one think that until now the poor child had been nameless and unclaimed, interchangeable with any other newborn. The family moved into this baptism with full force, ready to name and claim their own.

In fact, baptism overrode the claims of the formidable Cadigan clan, initiating Mary Charlotte into another family, the family of the "Children of God." Her parents had to hand the infant over to the celebrant, who received her on behalf of this other family. I hoped that the celebrant and new family would be appropriately appreciative of the antique dress. It must have been hard for the parents to listen to strangers making promises over their daughter, promises to rear her in the faith, promises to pray for her, promises to renounce the devil in "all his works and all his ways." Delicately but firmly, the celebrant divested Mary Charlotte of the heirloom dress, removing the claim of generations. As he plunged the infant naked into the font, her mother flinched. The celebrant then lifted the child, dripping wet, up in front of the assembly, pronouncing her "Child of God." Finally, the celebrant handed the child over to her godparents, who claimed Mary Charlotte on behalf of yet another family: the family of the Children of God.

The ceremony of baptism confounds us. Like the Cadigans, we prefer to play it as a christening or the conferral of a family name. In fact, baptism removes the infant from its family of origin and adopts it into a new one. The most important name conferred in baptism is not the family name, "Mary Charlotte Cadigan" or "Martha Ellen Stortz," but the name "Child of God." With baptism we receive a new identity, an identity that does not come with passport or ID card but with relationships. Within the horizon of baptism, *who* we are depends decisively on *whose* we are, and baptism signals new relationships of belonging to God and to Christ. The apostle Paul put these new relationships simply but powerfully: "You belong to Christ and Christ belongs to God"

(1 Corinthians 3:4). Relationships shape baptismal identity as God adopts us into a family of brothers and sisters in Christ. Living into these relationships, we live into the world according to God.

Baptismal ceremonies repeat ancient gestures of adoption, which a contemporary of Jesus' would have recognized immediately. It is easy to interpret these gestures as hand signals done for the benefit of the backbenchers and balcony-dwellers, but in fact these gestures bear greater significance. In the ancient world, lifting up a newborn was a way of claiming paternity. Immediately after its birth, an infant was presented to the presumed father of the child, and he could choose to lift the child up or not. With this gesture, the father claimed paternity, and the claimed child would rest secure in the family's embrace and inheritance. Unfortunately, not all newborns were lifted up. Children were routinely set down to die of exposure or to be picked up by others. The public squares of ancient cities had a customary spot, the *lactarium*, where unclaimed children were abandoned. They could be picked up by strangers and raised as slaves, servants, or prostitutes. Occasionally they were adopted by childless families as sons and daughters, heirs to the family wealth.

The social reality of children in the ancient world stands as a backdrop for the apostle Paul's letters to the earliest Christian communities. These communities regarded all newly baptized Christians, whether children or adults, as "infants," or *infantes*, in part because they were often abandoned by their biological families for following this new faith. These new Christians found themselves adopted by a new family in baptism. They were ceremonially lifted up and claimed as "Children of God." With God as their Father and Christ as their Brother, they became heirs to the kingdom of God. So claimed, these "Children of God" would be free from slavery and abandonment for all eternity. The apostle Paul alludes to these ancient practices of adoption in his discussion of baptism: "So you are no longer a slave but a child, and if a child then also an heir, through God" (Galatians 4:7); "For you did not receive a spirit of slavery to fall back into fear, but you have received a spirit of adoption. When we cry, 'Abba! Father!' it is that very Spirit bearing witness with our spirit that we are children of God, and if children, then heirs, heirs of God and joint heirs with Christ—if, in fact, we suffer with him so that we may also be glorified with him" (Romans 8:15–17).

An ancient reader would have supplied the gestures behind the texts. They surface in the familiar ceremony of baptism, which adopts us into a new family with God as our Father and Christ as our Brother.

What is that inheritance that membership in the new family guarantees us? We gain clues about our adoptive family from Jesus' baptism. As was the case with Mary Charlotte, baptism wrenched Jesus from his family of origin, repositioning him in relationship to a God who claimed him as Son. Until the time of his own baptism, Jesus had been a mere carpenter working in his family's business. He bore the name of his earthly father, Jesus bar Joseph. Jesus' baptism changed everything, giving him a new family business and revealing his true parentage. Baptism drew him into a new identity and a new vocation. Jesus lived out of his baptism; everything that followed began there.

Jesus' baptism was so important that the evangelist Mark began his Gospel with it. Mark avoided the lengthy genealogical digression that began Matthew's Gospel, as well as Luke's leisurely birth narrative and John's cosmic speculations. No "Once upon a time . . ." here. Mark stripped the story down to its basics, beginning his account with the announcement of Jesus' baptismal identity: "The beginning of the good news of Jesus Christ, the Son of God" (Mark 1:1). A mere nine verses later, we are at the River Jordan, where wilderness prophet John the Baptist prepared to baptize Jesus. The heavens opened, and a dove descended. A voice announced, "You are my Son, the Beloved; with you I am well pleased" (Mark 1:11). Mark launched his Gospel with Jesus' baptism, which inaugurated his public ministry and revealed Jesus as God's Son.

From the moment of baptism forward, Jesus addressed God as "Father," and this opened a new relationship to a God whom the Israelites had kept at arm's length. Because God claimed Jesus as Son, now Jesus—and the rest of us!—can claim God as Father. A new intimacy developed, and Jesus tended the relationship fiercely. He ditched his disciples to spend time with his Father; he wandered into the wilderness to talk with his Father; he climbed mountains to be alone with his Father. The way Jesus practiced his baptism give us clues about how we might practice ours.

As in any intimate relationship there are problems, and Jesus wrestled with his destiny and with what it meant to be Son of this Father. There were as many sharp exchanges as reassuring ones, as many hard words as loving ones. But the two remained faithful to one another. Even when Jesus accused his Father of abandoning him, the Father stood silent and suffering with him at the foot of the cross. A medieval fresco titled *The Trinity* by the fourteenth-century Italian artist Masaccio presents the Father's companionship beautifully. God the Son is crucified on the cross while God the Spirit descends upon the head of Jesus, as it did in Jesus' baptism. God the Father holds up both arms of the cross, leaning his head toward the Son in compassion. The Father accompanies the Son through death into resurrection.

"You are my Child, the Beloved; with you I am well pleased." We need to hear these words at every baptism that occurs in the name of the Triune God. Whether the candidate is old or young, whether baptism is chosen *by* the candidate or *for* her, God speaks these words to everyone in the ceremony of baptism. With these words, God claims each of us, giving us permission to claim God in turn. Like Jesus, we tend that relationship in prayer, spoken and unspoken. God the Father in turn tends the relationship. Just as the Father stood with Jesus in the crucifixion, He stands by us in our darkest moments. The Father even weathered the Son's cry of abandonment—"My God, my God, why have you forsaken me!"

The Father did not falter, and we know that we can do the same. Because we were lifted up in baptism and claimed as "Children of God," we remain safe from abandonment or slavery. We can count on God's love and constancy. Just as Jesus' baptism altered forever his relationship to God, so it alters ours. We too count on God's love, constancy, and claim on us as "Children."

"You are my Daughter, the Beloved; with you I am well pleased." The words give such life that a friend returns to them every day, making daily claim on a God who has already claimed her in baptism. She keeps a bowl of water on her dining room table. Every morning she plunges her hand into the water. She removes it to trace the sign of the cross on her forehead. Every evening before going to bed, she returns to the table to repeat the gesture. Morning and night she circles back to the same bowl of water and makes the same gesture. I asked her about it, and she replied, "It seems silly, but I want to remind myself of my baptism," she said. "I spend my days being so many things to so many people, I need to remember that in my heart of hearts, I'm the same person: a Child of God." As she makes her daily turn around the waters of baptism, my friend listens again for words spoken by the God who claims her.

God claims us as "Children," and God also claims us for the work of the kingdom. We receive an inheritance as joint heirs with Christ, and our work as his brothers and sisters is to carry on the family business. This inheritance is more than just a paper transaction, where we receive the franchise for the God business. We don't just pick up where Jesus left off; we become Jesus' body in the world, the ongoing presence of the incarnation. Baptism incorporates us into the body of Christ so that we become his crucified and resurrected body at work in the world today. It will mark us, as it marked Jesus' body. We may suffer as he did, but we know that we will be resurrected as he was. We may bear wounds on our bodies like the ones he bore on his, but we will participate in his resurrection. The apostle Paul put it well: "Do you not know that all of us who have been baptized into Christ Jesus were baptized into his death?

Therefore we have been buried with him by baptism into death, so that, just as Christ was raised from the dead by the glory of the Father, so we too might walk in newness of life" (Romans 6:3–4).

Paul reminded the community at Rome that as "Children of God," they were part of Christ's body. As the body of Christ, they had to suffer as Christ did. But as the body of Christ was raised up, so they would be raised up as well.

A small chapel at the Jesuit University in San Salvador, El Salvador, captures Paul's spirit. Around the sanctuary hang fourteen Stations of the Cross, but instead of featuring scenes from the passion of Christ, the Stations display drawings of the Salvadoran people, who were brutalized, tortured, and raped during the nation's civil war. The pictures commemorate Christians who carry on Christ's witness in the world, suffering as he suffered, lifted up in resurrection as he was.

Baptism incorporates them—and us—into the body of Christ. Where it goes, we will go. Through baptism, we become disciples who are Christ's body in the world: we become his feet and hands. As members of the body of Christ, we literally re-member that body in the world, bone on bone, sinew on sinew. Indeed, we may be the body of Christ that people first encounter, the body they long to touch.

Think about the body of Christ for a moment as a human body. Think of the marks that were on it at the time of Christ's death: marks in his feet and hands where nails were pounded, a mark in his side where a spear pierced him, the marks of the scourging he had received, bruises and cuts where he had been beaten. The apostle Thomas would not believe he was in the presence of the resurrected Christ until he touched that body. He wanted hands-on proof.

In our own contemporary generation of seekers, there are thousands like Thomas. They will not believe until they can touch the body of Christ. We should be the hands-on proof of the resurrection these seekers demand. In the concrete practice of baptism,

Christians re-member the body of Christ. We carry on the incarnation in the world today. This is what it means to be baptized into the body. We are the body Christ has in the world: we are Christ's hands.

I am the only pianist in the family, not because of my singular talent, but owing to a rather poignant misunderstanding. Piano lessons were offered to my younger sister, who declined, protesting "My hands don't know the right keys." She thought her fingers lacked the special intelligence that would send them scurrying gracefully across the keyboard. The truth is that none of us knows the right keys. That's why we circle back to baptism to listen again to the phrasing, learn the fingering, catch the tone of a difficult passage. Baptism is where we receive instruction from our older Brother Jesus, who assures us that despite all mistakes, we too are Children of God. God the Father will neither abandon nor dismiss us because God did not abandon his Son Jesus. So we continue as Christ's hands in the world and pray as the psalmist prayed: "Prosper for us the work of our hands. . . . O prosper the work of our hands" (Psalms 90:17). As Christ's hands in the world, we join a family business. We adopt family values that extend the Father's work into the world.

## Family Business and Family Values

My brother-in-law and his wife adopted two young girls from Guatemala, and they joined the family just in time for the annual Christmas Day dinner and exchange of gifts. My husband's family is large and boisterous, with lots of people, lots of laughter, and lots of volume. As people started arriving, the door would open to admit yet another wave of new aunts and uncles and cousins. The girls' eyes got bigger and bigger. They had never seen so many presents; they had never seen so many decorations on a Christmas tree; they had never seen so many pale-skinned people in one place at one time. Everyone wanted to welcome them to the family, and the onslaught of sheer goodwill was overwhelming.

Similarly, baptism not only introduces us to God as a Father and Jesus as our Brother; it serves up a whole new horde of brothers and sisters in Christ. The earliest Christian ceremonies demonstrated this powerfully. Baptisms were crowded events with a cast of candidates stretching across generations. The candidate had the sense of coming into a new family, and the congregation had the sense of welcoming new members into its midst. In these earliest ceremonies, no one could mistake baptism for a virtuoso event, the mark of one's own private spirituality. Baptism foreshadowed an important truth: discipleship would be a crowded undertaking.

At the same time, newly baptized Christians knew that there would be a community to sustain them, to guide them, and to accompany them along the way. Becoming a "Child of God" meant there were other children with whom one could play and with whom one had to get along. Becoming a "member of the body of Christ" meant there were other members, without which one would cease to function.

I remember my father-in-law declaiming at table: "Our friends we choose; our relatives are thrust upon us." We all looked at each other, wondering which of us he might be speaking about. In similar fashion, baptism thrusts upon us a new community of disciples. Through it we are incorporated into a new family, one that is not perfect by any means. As with any family, we are stuck with people we might not otherwise have chosen to be with. With all its flaws, though, the family of brothers and sisters in Christ forms the community where the call to discipleship is discerned and answered. We need this family—perhaps more than we know.

Baptism's family values reorganize family around the lines of promise rather than the lines of blood. How painful it must have been for Jesus' own siblings to go looking for him and finally get a message to him: "Your mother and your brothers are waiting outside, wanting to speak to you." Imagine their bewilderment when Jesus' words came back to them: "Here are my mother and my brothers! For whoever does the will of my Father in heaven is my brother and sister and mother".(Matthew 12:46–50; Mark 3:31–35; Luke 8:19–21). In baptism, old family ties give way to new ones.

At the same time, this new family of brothers and sisters in Christ could be great comfort in an uncertain world. In earliest Christianity, new Christians risked a great deal for their faith, everything from disinheritance to exile and death. Baptism initiated them into a welcoming family, one that stood ready to teach, feed, and support them in life and in death. Moreover, this new family of brothers and sisters in Christ crossed lines that had divided the ancient world into groups segregated by gender, class, profession, and ethnicity. Every station in life had a god or goddess who was particularly identified with the men and women of that caste. Mithras was the god of warriors; Ceres, the goddess of the farmers; Minerva, the goddess of the philosophers; Vesta Virginalis, the goddess of young unmarried women. Even prostitutes had their own goddess. The cults surrounding these gods and goddesses featured their own initiation rites, their own secret ceremonies, and their own sacred meals. There was a place for everyone—and everyone was supposed to stay in his or her ordained place.

Against the background of this tightly stratified society, the God of Jesus Christ seemed dangerously indiscriminate, as Paul expressed when he wrote to the Galatians: "There is no longer Jew or Greek, there is no longer slave or free, there is no longer male or female; for all of you are one in Christ" (Galatians 3:28). In Christ, all traditional boundaries vanished—and that simple fact threatened to disrupt the whole social order. Slaves came together with noblewomen to celebrate Christ's sacred meal. Farmhands mixed with former soldiers to be initiated into the Christian cult. Baptism created a community where all came together.

These motley communities seemed to like it that way. "Look at how they love one another!" sneered a Roman observer. Communities of Christians stunned people in a world where only like were supposed to associate with like, where people of different classes did not mingle, and where there was precious little love to go around. "Here," said Jesus emphatically, "are my mother and my sisters and my brothers." Through baptism, Christians practiced a new form of community, a dangerous community that cut across the boundaries of family and tribe, race and nationality, class and gender. In the movie *Romero,* there is a scene where Archbishop Oscar Romero meets with a wealthy family who had long been friends of his. A young woman in the family asks him to baptize her daughter in a private ceremony for family and relatives. Romero politely refuses, saying that baptisms must occur at the Sunday liturgy when all the faithful are present. The mother looks worried and then blurts out "But I don't want my daughter baptized with all those Indians!" Baptism creates a dangerous community where Ladinos mix with Indians, white with black and brown, slave with free. In baptism, we enter into the wild joy of all the "Children of God."

This new community of brothers and sisters in Christ has responsibilities outside the family. It is not enough—indeed, it has never been enough—just to take care of the family. As Christ's body in the world, baptized Christians may be the only way many people encounter Jesus. We may be their call to "follow me." As members of the body of Christ, Christians proclaim God's love to a world that is hungry for it.

Too often Christians display baptism as a badge of privilege, as if their cherished identities singled them out as the *only* beloved children of God. This understanding of baptism could not be further from the truth. In fact, by incorporating Christians into the body of God's beloved Son, baptism drafts us as witnesses to God's love for the whole world. Disciples continue the incarnation by embodying God's love for the world.

Baptism makes Christians ambassadors of the incarnation. Their posts are in the world, and they fan out to heal, to witness, and to serve. A large congregation in the Pacific Northwest captured the dynamic of discipleship in its mission statement: "Gathered to worship; scattered to serve." Jesus' baptism inaugurated his *public* ministry, not his work among the people of his own kind. Jesus ministered outside the boundaries of first-century Judaism. We find him talking with "outcasts and sinners," healing among the Roman oppressors, traveling through the no-man's land of Samaria. Disciples who follow in Jesus' footsteps find themselves ministering "outside the box."

Disciples are "scattered to serve." They return to church for worship and praise, but their journey does not end there. The world is the field of their mission, so that it can become a world according to God. The trajectory of discipleship swings from the baptismal font into the world—and back again. Often the disciples serve unnoticed. In his book *Life Together*, Dietrich Bonhoeffer observed that it's far more important to talk to Christ about the unbeliever than to talk to the unbeliever about Christ.[1] Prayer to Christ on behalf of the neighbor counts as an act of quiet resistance in a world that overvalues accomplishment. Feeling helpless as the nation careened toward war in Iraq, one of my colleagues asked an activist, "What can I do?" He wanted to be doing something, and surely an activist would know what that might be. The activist regarded the man thoughtfully for a moment and then said, "Pray. That's what you can do. That's what you people do best, and that's what we need now." My colleague was dumbfounded, but after he thought about it for a while, prayer seemed exactly the right thing to do. He organized a prayer chain on the Internet that reached thousands of people all over the country. For prayer works less by doing than by undoing. With prayer, we find our hands unclenching. We loosen our grip on prestige or power or gain, whether it be personal, national, or international. The advice of this activist morphed into a powerful witness of prayer. As people around the country joined in this prayer, they offered intercession for the world—not just the Christian world, but for "all the children of the world" of whatever nation, color, or creed.

"He's got the whole world in his hands," the refrain of an old campfire song runs. Recalling God's hands-on history with the

whole of creation, Christians know that we are not the only children in God's hands. God promised in a rainbow never again to
destroy the world by water, and the promise includes all creatures,
not just a few select tribes or species (Genesis 9:1–17). God
promised that Abraham would be the "ancestor of a multitude of
nations," not just a privileged few (Genesis 17:5). While celebrating God as our Father and Christ as our Brother, we "Children of
God" pray for all the children of the world. Baptism drafts us into
a service of love that extends beyond the family of brothers and
sisters in Christ and into the world. After all, the Bible tells us that
God "so loved the world" (John 3:16), not just the baptized. Jesus
came into the world as God's messenger of love. As his body in
the world today, Christians carry on with the family business
Jesus started.

Every Christmas resurrects the perennial campaign to "bring
Christ back into Christmas." Christians disgusted with the commercialism of Christmas came up with a catchy phrase, complete
with bumper stickers and buttons, to remind everyone that "Jesus
is the reason for the season." Maybe this begs the question a bit:
What is the reason for Jesus? The answer is simple: to show the
world God's love. If baptism makes Christians part of the body of
the beloved Son, it also makes them witnesses to the divine love
affair God has with the whole of creation.

Every Christmas Eve my pastor tells the same story to the families assembled on that most holy of nights. It is the story of another
family on another Christmas Eve. Wind buffeted their home with
a combination of snow and sleet and ice. The mother set out for
midnight Mass with her son. As they did every year, they entreated
the father to accompany them. And as he did every year, the father
declined. Politely but firmly, he explained again that he found the
whole notion of Christmas bizarre. He simply could not fathom a
God who loved human beings enough to become one of them. The
mother and son departed, and the father remained at home, alone
in the storm.

As he waited by the fire, the man looked outside to find a flock of birds alighting on the lawn. They huddled against the wind, but their wings quickly encrusted with ice. They could not fly, and the man knew that by morning the cold would kill them. The man went outside, opening the door of the barn to shoo them inside, where it was dry and warm enough for their wings to thaw. But the birds ran from him, scattering in various directions. He tried everything he could think of to get the birds into the barn, but the birds would not be herded. Defeated, he returned to the warmth of his house. "If I were just one of them, I could show them the way out of danger." He caught himself short: he had stumbled on the truth of the Christmas message. He ran up against the "reason for the season." God so loves the world that God became one of us. As members of the body of Christ, baptized Christians witness that enduring love for "all the children of the world."

# 4

The Lord's Supper

*Sustaining the Body of Christ*

A few blocks in downtown Berkeley, California, are known to residents as "Gourmet Gulch." On one side of the street is restaurant guru Alice Walker's internationally known establishment, Chez Panisse. On the other is an employee-owned and -operated food collective dating back to the sixties, the Cheeseboard Cooperative, which boasts of fresh baked goods and cheeses from all over the world. Around lunchtime the smell of newly baked Cheeseboard pizzas wafts down the street as people line up outside an old storefront for lunch, while inside a local musician plunks away on an upright piano. A fresh produce store anchors the block, and anyone needing to refuel can pick up a cappuccino at the French Hotel, where the radiant Mexican American Angel pumps espresso and dispenses smiles.

The creed of these "foodies" seems self-evident: "You are what you eat." Standing in line for coffee at the French Hotel, patrons place their orders in paragraphs: "I'll have a no-foam, no-fat, soymilk double decaf latte." If you happen to eavesdrop on a conversation in Gourmet Gulch, it is likely to be about food or diet, conducted with a religious fervor. The Protestant reformers felt that one was "justified by grace through faith." In this part of the world, people are justified by diet.

The notion that you are what you eat was even truer in the ancient world, where *what* you ate—and *with whom*—marked class, gender, race, and country of origin. One of Greek philosopher Plato's most famous dialogues, "The Symposium," took place at a feast. Plato considered a meal to be the perfect staging area for a lively discussion on the nature of love. Centuries later, philosopher, statesman, and emperor Marcus Aurelius revealed in his *Soliloquies* a fastidious attention to diet as a way of life. The Hebrew scriptures regulated what went into the mouths of God's chosen people, in part to set them apart from the tribes surrounding them and in part because diet also did the internal work of purification. What they ate distinguished the Jews as people of a different God.

In the midst of cultures that cultivated diet as a spiritual practice, the dining habits of Christians came under close scrutiny. The New Testament shows that people at that time found the diets of Christians threatening to the social order. Jesus failed to follow the strict dietary codes, refused to adhere to the complex religious rituals of cleansing that preceded a meal, and ate and drank with all the wrong kinds of people. Again and again in the Gospels, he is accused of being "a glutton, a drunkard, a friend of tax collectors and sinners" (Matthew 11:19). Jesus flung a final insult at a culture obsessed with diet as a spiritual practice: Jesus offered himself as food. What kind of diet is this?

This chapter explores the significance of the practice of sharing the body and blood of Jesus, known as Holy Communion or the Eucharist or the Lord's Supper. Christian churches celebrate this sacred meal as a part of their worship, though they differ in how often they do so and how they understand it. The Lord's Supper counts as a core ritual in the Christian ethos; it is also a practice. Then as now, disciples "are what they eat." Feeding on Christ, disciples become his body in a world that hungers for his presence. The Lord's Supper is a three-course meal within an elaborate ritual of blessing. It is first and foremost food that is not simply eaten but shared. Second, the Lord's Supper is holy food, nourishing disciples with Jesus' body and blood. Finally, it stands as a practice of blessing in the midst of a banquet of beggars.

## Eucharistic Generosity

Several years ago in Milwaukee, Wisconsin, a young man who was also a lapsed Catholic approached the bishop of that diocese. He wanted to reconnect to the church of his childhood. "What must I do to become a Catholic?" he asked. The bishop paused for a moment and then answered, "Go to mass every Sunday, and work in a soup kitchen every week. Come back in six months, and let's talk." The bishop did not recommend reading the Baltimore Catechism or the whole of the Bible from Genesis straight through to Revelation. He urged the young man to participate every week in two meals: one at Mass, the other in a soup kitchen. What is the connection between these two meals?

Both meals feature food that is shared among people. The Lord's Supper does not invite congregants to swarm the altar, tear off a chunk of bread, and wash it down with a slug of wine. Rather the celebrant blesses bread and wine with Jesus' words, breaks bread, pours wine, and presents it to people who come forward with empty hands. In some congregations the celebrant sends the food out into the midst of the people, who pass it around to one another. Fed by one neighbor, people turn and feed another. People share food that was shared with them.

The Lord's Supper works like a soup kitchen, and similar gestures surface. After the meal is blessed, volunteers ladle food into plates that hungry people bring forward. They pour drink into cups that thirsty people present. Sometimes food comes directly to the table, and people serve each other family-style. In both the meal at the altar and the meal in the soup kitchen, the choreography is the same. Food is not simply eaten but shared. The good bishop from Milwaukee hoped that the young man would find a symmetry of sharing in the two meals.

When I was a child growing up in one of Baltimore's brick row houses, a neighborhood mother used to summon her hungry family to dinner by calling up and down the alley, "Come and get it!"

Appearing out of nowhere, children scrambled in the back door to take what they could. Dining was apparently about "getting it," not "giving it," about taking and not sharing food. For this family, the Lord's Supper would have required remarkable restraint. Unlike a family supper, which was "taken by you," the Lord's Supper was "given for you." Those three words sum up the countercultural character of this meal. These three words free us from the "Mine!" fields. They liberate me from enslavement to everything I consider rightly mine by dint of hard work, earned compensation, or entitlement. The Lord's Supper shares food that is given for me, not taken by me as my just due.

Several years ago an older woman from my neighborhood in Oakland appeared at my door with her arms full of roses, "Here, I'm giving you some roses. I have more than I need." I love roses, and I wonder how anyone could have too many of them. I knew that Eleanor loved roses too. But more than she loved the roses, she loved bestowing them by the bucketful on her neighbors. Her generosity conspired with the generosity of the rosebush itself to keep me in roses all summer. Clipping the buds only produced more. Her roses bloomed long past their season—and everyone in the neighborhood reaped the abundance.

Long ago Eleanor found her way out of the "Mine!" fields, that prison of feeling that certain things belonged to her. She felt that the roses were not hers to begin with, nor did she think that her expert care entitled her to their beauty. They came unbidden. She received them; she tended them; she gave them away. She even gave away her generosity, crediting the roses with magnanimity: "They are such generous flowers." Eleanor felt the roses were no more her own than the sunlight that filled her yard. She gave them away with delight.

The distance between giving and taking is the difference between an open hand and a clenched fist. That distance creates a space where miracles happen, whether they occur in a soup kitchen or a church sanctuary. Miracles happen wherever food is shared, as a miraculous meal from the Bible demonstrates. The feeding of the five thousand features prominently in all four Gospels. The fact that all four accounts, written by different authors to different communities at different times, agree on head count (five thousand), the original number of loaves and fishes (five and two, respectively), and the twelve baskets of leftovers, is a tiny miracle in itself (Matthew 14:13–21; Mark 6:32–33; Luke 9:10–17; John 6:1–15). This whole miracle of feeding happened because a small boy broke out of the "Mine!" fields.

The disciples found themselves in a deserted place with night falling and thousands of people in their charge. They went to Jesus wondering what to do, and he told them to feed the crowd. They protested that they had no food, and Jesus asked them to bring whatever they could scrounge together. They found a young boy with provisions, and he shared them, giving the disciples five barley loaves and two fish. In gestures he would use at his final meal with the disciples, Jesus blessed the bread, broke it, and shared it with the disciples. Then they shared the food with the crowd. Five thousand people ate their fill; twelve baskets of food were left over—all because a young boy did not declare his simple meal "Mine!"

I have always felt that this miracle was misnamed, passed on by someone more impressed with quantity rather than the rare virtue of generosity. The accurate title would be something like "a little boy shares his food" or "sharing food with the five thousand hungry people" or simply "the miraculous sharing." Whatever the title, this miracle stands as the first recorded soup kitchen in the ancient world. It foreshadows the Last Supper, where Jesus shared himself as bread and wine, presenting his own body as food and his own blood as drink. The young boy gave up his food, and Jesus gave up his life to feed his friends. Disciples were supposed to see a symmetry of sharing between "the miraculous sharing" and the Last Supper.

The Last Supper functions as an afterimage of the miraculous sharing of food. As he did when he fed five thousand hungry people, Jesus blessed this final meal and gave it to the disciples. He did not take bread, bless it, and break it only to feed himself. Jesus shared the bread he blessed. Jesus returned after his resurrection to dine again with the disciples. At that meal, he directed the disciples to a ministry of sharing food: "Feed my lambs; . . . feed my sheep" (John 21:15–17). In a very real sense, Jesus set in motion a miraculous chain of events that continues today as disciples share the food we have received with others. The meal continues until we reach the hungriest mouth in the world. Shared food nourishes disciples along the way; sharing food becomes our mission. Like the loaves and fishes at the miraculous feeding, the food disciples share will have no end, for we share the endless goodness of Christ.

Christ's endless goodness is often depicted as an endless feast, and many descriptions of eternal life depict an eschatological banquet. As a modern parable describes this feast, it will be open to everyone, regardless of whether they are seated in heaven or in hell. In hell the inmates gather around a stupendous banquet with fabulous food and drink. There is only one thing wrong: the utensils the guests use to feed themselves are two feet long. There is no way they can reach their mouths with such elongated forks, and the scene at the table is one of pandemonium as the guests first complain and then physically fall to blows in their frustration. In heaven the residents gather around the same stupendous banquet at a table groaning with every good thing. The table is set with the same large utensils, but the guests dine with pleasure. The forks and spoons reach easily across the table, and guests feed each other. They can eat the meal because they share it. They don't even think about what they are supposed to do. Eucharistic practice shapes a spirit of eucharistic generosity. Disciples share food because that is simply who they are. Just as Eleanor credits her generosity to the roses, these tablemates credit their generosity to the Lord's Supper. Jesus' magnanimity created their own, and now sharing is what they do. The sharing goes deeper than that: generosity is who they are. They practice eucharistic generosity.

Four very different meals—the miraculous sharing, the Lord's Supper, the soup kitchen, and the imagined heavenly banquet—all feature sharing of food, and I suspect that the bishop wanted the young man to understand their similarity. But the Lord's Supper stands out because this meal is not only about sharing food but also about the food that is shared. In this meal, disciples find food that will sustain us for the journey ahead. This food so satisfies that we cannot help but share it with others. This food is Jesus' body, the "living water," the "bread from heaven," the "true vine."

## Jesus Himself as Holy Food

Contemporary scientific debate swirls around the human genome, which geneticists have finally mapped. Genetic code predisposes people to everything from disease to levels of intelligence to physical characteristics. How much of someone's behavior can we attribute to genes? Can environmental factors, background, even parenting practices alter genetic predisposition? Nature versus nurture debates rage as scientists struggle to understand how genetics hardwires human behavior. The creed genetic science espouses could be summed up as the conviction that "you are what your genes dictate."

As we have seen, in the ancient world, people believed that "you are what you eat." This conviction directed ancient science. Indeed, the science of medicine developed to explore the impact of diet on health. Food hardwired people, and classical literature prescribed food and drink appropriate to body type, gender, general condition of the body, and the activities that occupied one's time. As part of a general concern for purity, the Hebrews formulated dietary laws that listed animals that could and could not be eaten as food (Leviticus 11; Deuteronomy 14:3–20). Other ancient Near Eastern peoples fashioned similar codes of their own. Because pigs ate carrion and cannibalized each other, they were classified as "unclean." Diet segregated tribes and classes of people; it separated rich and poor. Different groups of people had access to different kinds of food; they participated in very different dietary regimes, some out of necessity, some by choice. In a culture obsessed with eating and drinking the right kinds of food, Jesus' dining habits caused a great deal of controversy.

As we see in the Gospel of John, Jesus consistently provoked the staunch defenders of strict dietary regimes with claims that he had food for all kinds of people. He announced to a Samaritan woman that he could find her "living water" (John 7:30), and water was one of the most precious commodities in a desert climate. Moreover, Jesus offered this precious commodity to a woman. In a society that strictly segregated people by gender, a man did not even address a woman in public, much less offer her something to drink. To further outrage his followers, Jesus offered water not just to any woman but to a woman who was Samaritan, a people despised by the Jews. Finally, the Samaritan woman confessed that she lived with a man who was not her husband, and by religious reckoning that made her a sinner. The whole encounter outraged Jesus' own people—even his disciples were "astonished" (John 4:27). Jesus promised heavenly food, "living water," to someone far outside the flock.

The provocation intensified. Immediately after his encounter with the Samaritan woman, Jesus' disciples reminded him that he must be hungry: "Rabbi, eat something" (John 4:31). Still stung by his offer to an outsider, they calibrated their remarks to remind Jesus that a rabbi ought to be more careful in his dining habits. Jesus refused their counsel: "I have food to eat that you do not know about" (John 4:32). He fed from a heavenly supply of food, and his diet changed him, setting him increasingly apart from the surrounding population.

Jesus' choice in dining companions also set him outside local custom. When he dined, he chose to eat with people the authorities deemed "unclean," "unworthy," or "sinful." Jesus shunned polite company to eat with outcasts and sinners, sharing their lot. Some of these outsiders were impoverished and could not afford the

Temple sacrifices that would have cleansed them; others did work despised by an occupied people, like collecting taxes for the Romans.

Jesus' dining practices and his tablemates alike brought censure. Again and again people commented: "Look, a glutton and a drunkard, a friend of tax collectors and sinners!" (Matthew 11:19). The words refer not to any intemperance on Jesus' part but to his tablemates. He ate and drank with the wrong kinds of people. Sharing a table meant sharing life. Friends not only dined together; they shared their lives. In eating and drinking with outcasts and sinners, Jesus signaled his willingness to share his life with them. Jesus' table etiquette gained him notoriety.

Eventually, Jesus took his dining practices to the extreme. He went beyond dining with people and sharing his life with them; he demonstrated his willingness to give up his life for his friends. Jesus offered *himself* as food. He claimed he was "the bread of life" (John 6:35), and he promised that those who ate this bread would become his body. The crowd following him was so offended by these words that many of them left: "Because of this many of his disciples turned back and no longer went about with him" (John 6:66). Each time in John's Gospel that Jesus proclaimed himself as food or drink, either "the Passover of the Jews was near" (John 2:13) or the leader of another dietary regime was lurking in the wings to overhear his outrageous claim. This was no coincidence. Jesus' offer of himself as food and drink threatened to upset the social order.

Jesus served as the mainstay of the disciples' diet. Jesus was food; Jesus was drink. These claims overturned the logic of the Passover meal, whose rituals repeated the meal that nurtured the Israelites as they fled from Egypt. Jesus provocatively restructured this ritual meal so that he himself was the Passover lamb and he himself was the Passover wine. When word spread of Jesus' final meal with his disciples, his identification with these key ritual elements of the meal deeply offended religious authorities. Although this final meal did not lead directly to the crucifixion, it is no coincidence that crucifixion followed immediately afterward. For religious authorities who regulated food and diet, the Last Supper was the last straw.

The Last Supper drew all kinds of people together around a common meal with a single menu. It hardwired everyone in ways that today would be like surgically reconfiguring our genetic code. All kinds of people, whatever their gender, tribe, or genetic code, would be made one through this supernatural nourishment. Surprisingly, the account of the Last Supper in John's Gospel does not focus on food. John does not speak the familiar "words of institution" in his account of the Last Supper: "This is my body that is for you. Do this in remembrance of me. This cup is the new covenant in my blood. Do this, as often as you drink it in remembrance of me" (1 Corinthians 11:24–25). In John's Gospel, Jesus has already spoken these words when he claimed to be "living water" for a Samaritan woman, when he claimed to be "the bread of life" for his disciples. He promises to all who feed from him: "Those who eat my flesh and drink my blood abide in me, and I in them" (John 6:56). John has already sated his audience with accounts of Jesus as holy food. Now he offers an account of feet, and footwashing functions as a kind of eucharistic parable.

In biblical times, footwashing always preceded a fine meal. The host never performed this task but assigned it to a servant. In John's account of the Last Supper, Jesus performed the task himself, preparing the disciples for the meal that would sustain them for the rest of their journey. As Jesus bent to wash their feet, the disciples protested. They argued among themselves; they peppered Jesus with questions. Nonetheless, these friends with whom Jesus dined gradually became Christ's body in the world. I have always wondered what happened to change the clueless and squabbling followers of the Synoptic Gospels into the fearless leaders of Acts of the Apostles. They seem like different people entirely—almost as if they'd had genetic surgery.

Through eating and drinking the body and blood of Christ, the disciples changed. Gradually they became what they had eaten; they turned into the body of Christ in the world. The apostle Paul put the transformation eloquently: "The cup of blessing that we bless, is it not a sharing in the blood of Christ? The bread that we break, is it not a sharing in the body of Christ? Because there is one bread, we who are many are one body, for we all partake of one bread" (2 Corinthians 10:16–17).

The body of Christ fashions a community into Christ's body in the world. As Christ's body, we reach deep into the heart of the world to touch the people Jesus touched, to teach the people he taught, and to dine with the people he dined with. We bring God's blessing to the world.

## A Practice of Blessing in a Banquet of Beggars

At Jesus' celebration of the Passover feast with his disciples, the Last Supper was preceded by traditional blessings. Jesus gave thanks for the food before he shared it. He offered the ancient Jewish prayer of thanksgiving that accompanied the feast: "Blessed are you, O Lord our God, King of the Universe." Longer eucharistic prayers still paraphrase these words, linking the Lord's Supper to countless thanksgivings for manna in the desert, for water from the rock, for other more ordinary offerings of food and drink at a daily table.

To understand eucharistic living and to grasp the Lord's Supper as a practice, we need to know how blessings work and why they are so closely related to thanksgiving. I was taught a very important lesson in blessing by my two Guatemalan nieces. When they joined us for their first family Christmas, they knew almost no English. In anticipation of the exchange of presents, they had been carefully taught to say, "Thank you," which they pronounced over and over again with great care.

My husband and I arrived at the gathering with presents for them, and we watched as the two opened their gifts. They burrowed through layers of wrapping paper and feet of ribbon, all the while repeating their mantra of thanksgiving: "Thank you thank you thank you thank you." There was real delight as they finally got inside their gifts. But then they turned to my husband and me, and a chorus of blessing began: "Thank *you* thank *you* thank *you!*" They began with thanksgiving for the gift; then they turned to bless the givers. They stumbled over reams of wrapping paper to give us both a big hug. It was gracious lesson in blessing.

Every thanksgiving gives thanks to someone for something, and the girls thanked us for their bright Christmas gifts. They moved from thanksgiving into blessing with the words "thank *you!*" It was a delight to us, because we had put something of ourselves into their gift. We had racked our brains trying to figure out what they might enjoy that would not presume English-language skills or First World cultural habits. We had adorned their gifts with small toys and bright bows. In presenting the gifts to the girls, we shamelessly made fun of our own poor Spanish-speaking skills. Behind these gifts were the givers, and the girls saw that immediately. Their "thank *you!*" was our blessing.

Though not the same, thanksgiving and blessing are closely related. We give thanks for the many gifts we have received, but once we turn from the gift to praise the giver, we move into the realm of blessing. The Lord's Supper entwines both thanksgiving and blessing. In giving thanks for the bread and wine, Jesus identified himself as both gift and giver. "Take; this is my body. This is my blood of the covenant, which is poured out for many" (Mark 14:22–23). The bread was his body; the wine was his blood. The gift did not merely symbolize the giver; rather, in this meal, the gift became the giver. In Jesus, blessing and thanksgiving converge and become one.

Jesus instructed the disciples to eat "in remembrance" of him. Anytime they shared this meal, they were to give thanks for the gift; they were to bless the giver. In sharing the Lord's Supper, the disciples replayed this complex ritual in which the gift becomes the giver. As they ate and drank, they participated again in the blessing that Jesus was to them—and continues to be to all people.

In feeding off Jesus' body and blood, we disciples today give thanks for the gift and bless the giver. In becoming what we eat, we are made a blessing for the world.

Most biblical blessings participate in this spiral of abundance. Biblical blessings turn from the gift to the giver, the One from whom all things come. My favorite blessing is the blessing from Psalm 103: "Bless the Lord, O my soul, and all that is within me, bless his holy name." This is the prayer I wake up with. As I stumble from sleep into waking, these words orient my being to the One who directs my days. At least that is my fervent hope. Some days hope fades fast as my soul crowds with classes to prepare, articles to write, meetings to negotiate, and people to meet. I need God's holy name to order my unholy clutter. These words remind me of all that I have to be thankful for: family, work, and friends, even my unholy clutter. Everything I have and everything I am I owe to God, and I stand in gratitude before the mystery of blessing and being blessed.

"And all that is within me, bless his holy name." The verse moves from thanksgiving directly to blessing as I name the One in whom I live and move and have my being. It is what I would call a "full-body blessing." I bless God not by going through the motions but by mobilizing every fiber of my being. Perhaps Jesus thought of these words as he gave thanks for food and blessed the giver of every good gift. Beneath thanksgiving and blessing we hear the steady pulse of the psalm: "Bless the Lord, O my soul, and all that is within me, bless his holy name." Though the disciples do not yet realize it, Jesus gives them his life. "All that is within him" he delivers to the disciples as food for the journey. As they feed off him, they will be both nourished and blessed. As they turn to the tasks of their discipleship in the world, they share the blessing that they have received.

"Bless the Lord, O my soul," the psalmist entreats centuries of believers. Does God need our blessings? Does it matter? What matters is that blessing God is as necessary to us as the food we eat and the air we breathe. We need to bless God for three reasons. First, we need to bless God because that is who we are. Otherwise we get profoundly lost in labyrinths of our own creation. Created in the image of God, we are hardwired to bless the One who made us. Like ducklings imprinted on their mother, we would follow God around in a sturdy little line were it not for the unholy clutter that gets in the way. In blessing God, we clear the decks and raze the rubble that blocks us from following the One whose nature we share.

Second, we bless God because that is *whose* we are. We belong to God, as the apostle Paul reminded his rowdy crowd in Corinth: "You belong to Christ, and Christ belongs to God" (1 Corinthians 3:23). Baptism incorporates us into the body of Christ, but the Lord's Supper nourishes us, transforming us into what we feed on. "You are what you eat!" is never truer than in the Eucharist. As we eat and drink the body and blood of Christ, we become a different kind of people.

Finally, we bless God because we have been blessed. We give thanks for our gifts, and we bless the Giver. In these simple acts of gratitude and blessing, we share our bounty with others. God carries our blessings forward into the whole of creation, like the ripples that spread out from a stone thrown into the stillness of a pond.

Blessings, especially biblical blessings, are leaky. They exceed the limits of reciprocity, which indicates a simple exchange. Reciprocity means that I give you something and you give me something back. I give you ten dollars; you give me a bouquet of tulips. This is not a blessing but a business transaction. Blessings are not about "payback." Instead, they are paid forward, out to all the world and forward to all generations. My parents gave me everything: love, education, safety, security, life itself. I could no more begin to pay them back than I could grow feathers and learn to fly. What I can do is give life, love, safety, and security to the next generation of children. What I can do is create the conditions for the next generation to flourish, and in so doing I let my blessings sweeten someone else's life. We pay our blessings forward by divine command. Jesus did not exhort disciples to "love *me* as I have loved you"; rather he urged them to "love *one another* as I have loved you" (John 13:34). Biblical blessings move beyond mere reciprocity to infuse everything with divine graciousness.

Two biblical figures demonstrate the bounty of biblical blessings. Abraham offered hospitality to three angels, and God blessed him in return. It looks like a simple exchange, but God was not merely promising Abraham that things would go well for him. God told Abraham that "all the nations of the earth shall be blessed in him" (Genesis 18:18; see also Genesis 12:3). Abraham's bounty would touch all people. The universal reach of Abraham's blessing made him the father of all believers. The apostle Paul claims that "all the Gentiles shall be blessed in you" (Galatians 3:18).

Mary, the mother of Jesus, stands as another example of the bounty of biblical blessings. Mary's kinswoman Elizabeth had been blessed in her old age with a child. Inspired by the Holy Spirit, she in turn blessed Mary: "Blessed are you among women, and blessed is the fruit of your womb" (Luke 1:42). Mary responded with her own blessing, which extended the blessings even further. She realized that "from now on all generations shall call me blessed" (Luke 1:48). As she counted the ways in which "the Mighty One" would carry her blessing forward, she suddenly saw that she received the ripple effect of Abraham's blessing. Overwhelmed with praise, she blessed God:

> His mercy is for those who fear him
> from generation to generation.
> He has shown strength with his arm;
> He has scattered the proud in the thoughts of the hearts.
> He has brought down the powerful from their thrones,
> and lifted up the lowly;
> He has filled the hungry with good things,
> and sent the rich away empty.
> He has helped his servant Israel,
> in remembrance of his mercy,
> According to the promise he made to our ancestors,
> to Abraham and to his descendants forever [Luke 1:46–55].

Abraham's blessing extended through time and space to embrace a young pregnant teenager. Mary testified that the blessings would not stop with her but would reach out to the lowly, the hungry, and the least fortunate.

Biblical blessings leak, and the ones offered in the Lord's Supper are perhaps the leakiest. Jesus blesses disciples with himself as heavenly food. He presents himself as both Gift and Giver. How do we live out the blessings we have received?

## Eucharistic Living

A good friend of mine lost her husband quite suddenly. In the weeks after his death, she began to lose weight as well. Her concerned friends descended on her bearing casseroles and questions. Was she sick? Was she depressed? Had she lost the will to live? She shrugged off our questions and made us take home our casseroles. "It's not a big problem. I just hate eating alone," she said. "I mean, what's the point? So if you're going to bring me food, be prepared to stay and share it with me." The widow taught us all an important lesson: eating is fundamentally a social act. Someday scientists and dietitians will prove that she is right. Food tastes better in the company of others. Something in the chemistry of eating together enhances a meal. The flavors blend better; the spices are more vivid.

We forget the social dimension of eating in a fast-food culture. We drive-through and eat-on-the-run so that we don't have to "waste time" preparing a meal. Many families rarely sit down at a table together to share a meal, given the balance of soccer games and piano lessons and PTA meetings and business trips. The Lord's Supper calls halt to all fast-food dining by inviting us to slow down and to sit down. We flourish in the company of others, for God blesses us in and through our neighbors—the blessings they bring and the food they share.

The message of eucharistic living goes deeper. Fast-food dining fuels fast-food spirituality, as shelf upon shelf of self-help books witness. There's a limit on how much we can help ourselves, no matter how well read we are. Like the widow, we depend on our friends for food and companionship. Their presence blesses us immeasurably, for they are both kindred spirits and the presence of God's Spirit. God blesses us with and through others, using their presence to bear the divine.

A friend who had visited Calcutta spoke of his experience navigating a busy street in the downtown area amid a sea of outstretched hands. Beggars lined the sidewalk, and he could not move without someone shoving a hand in his face, asking for a coin, a scrap of food, or a blessing. He was shocked at the level of suffering and need, at the way other pedestrians moved through the crowd ignoring the hands in front of them. But he was also jolted by the revelation that we are all beggars, dependent on neighbors for food, for friendship, for blessing. The people in front of him were under no illusion that they could make it on their own. They needed the kindness of strangers in order to survive. But don't we all? My friend gave what coins he had to the people in front of him, and as he emptied his pockets, he gave thanks for the people who had blessed him in times of need and in times of abundance.

The world according to God is a social reality, pointing us all toward a final banquet when all the children of the world will sit at table to break bread and drink wine together. Eucharistic living nurtures disciples in the meantime, teaching us to move through the world with open hands as we give and receive both blessings and bread.

# 5

## Prayer

### Conversations Along the Way

L ord, teach us to pray" (Luke 11:1). The disciples watched as Jesus excused himself from his crowds and his followers to find a quiet place to pray. When he returned, they begged him: "Teach us to pray." Their request seems odd. The disciples were good Jews, and part of their piety involved regular prayer. They had been taught prayers, and they knew where to direct them. Why ask for more?

The disciples wanted to encounter the God to whom Jesus prayed. This was a God whose name was so sacred the Jews did not pronounce it, speaking instead a substitute title like "Lord." Jesus not only spoke God's name but addressed God intimately, as "Abba" or "Father." The disciples wanted to be introduced to the God with whom Jesus was on such close terms. Maybe they felt that Jesus had somehow cracked the mystery of prayer.

Of course, no one ever cracks the mystery of prayer, even the great mystics. Prayer is not a means to an end; as a practice, it is an end in itself. Indeed, prayer is one of the core Christian practices. All of the practices of discipleship open us for relationship with the One who calls us. Prayer is a way of responding to that relationship; prayer listens for the One who calls. Like every relationship, the relationship with God needs tending; like every relationship, the one with God changes.

## Tending and Attending

"You never listen to me! Pay attention!" These are common refrains to any relationship that exists over time and space, whether between parent and child, husband and wife, or life partners who know each other's every move. The complaint masks a longing to be understood, heard deeply, and respected. One of the foremothers of the feminist movement, Nelle Morton, found that the first work of consciousness raising was the practice of attention. In countless women's groups, she discovered that people spoke when—and only when—they felt that whatever they had to say would be received. In fact, an atmosphere of respectful receptivity brought people out. Women said things they had not even known they were thinking. Morton described the practice of paying attention as "hearing someone to speech." People yearned for it, regardless of gender. When the disciples asked Jesus, "Teach us to pray," they revealed their desire for a relationship with God like his own, one characterized by a practice of deep listening or attention. Every relationship flourishes in an environment of attention, and the relationship described by prayer is no different.

A Buddhist monk asked his abbot to reveal to him the three secrets of contemplation. The abbot nodded and replied, "Attention, attention, attention." Like the monk, we may furrow our brow at this reply, but attention paves the way to prayer. Martin Luther offered an earthy description of attention. He wished that he could pray the way his dog sat next to the dinner table waiting for a bone. We can almost see the hungry animal panting and straining every muscle for any morsel that might drop from the dinner table. This is attention. Twentieth-century French philosopher Simone Weil offers another concrete exercise in paying attention: doing homework. She was a schoolteacher, and she had both assigned homework and done it herself. She found it a way of cultivating the habit of mind and heart so central to prayer. She writes of "a way of giving our attention to the data of a problem in geometry without trying to find the solution or to the words of a Latin or Greek text without trying to arrive at the meaning, a way of waiting, when we are writing, for the right word to come of itself at the end of our pen, while we merely reject all inadequate words."[1] Weil spoke of an openness in this kind of attention, a willingness not to rush to quick solutions or premature closure. School exercises, she firmly believed, prepared her students for prayer. Above all, prayer consists in paying attention.

The Old Testament underscores the importance of paying attention. Throughout the psalms and the prophets, the people of God plead: "Hearken to us!" This is the same refrain heard in any close relationship: "You never listen to me!" The book of the prophet Isaiah begins with a vision that begs to be noticed: "Hear, O heavens, and listen, O earth; for the Lord has spoken" (Isaiah 1:2). The psalms ring the changes on this familiar cry: "My God, my God, why have you forsaken me? Why are you so far from helping me, from the words of my groaning? O my God, I cry by day, but you do not answer" (Psalms 22:1–2). "Hear, O my people, and I will speak, O Israel, I will testify against you" (Psalms 50:7–8). "I sought the Lord, and he answered me, and delivered me from all my foes. . . . This poor soul cried, and was heard by the Lord, and was saved from every trouble" (Psalms 34:4, 6). These pleas for attention roll out in sheer poetry.

God demands that we pay attention as well. As the Old Testament depicts the relationship between God and God's people, paying attention is not a one-sided deal. The Shema, that great creed of Deuteronomy, makes this explicit at the outset: "Hear, O Israel" (Deuteronomy 6:4). God challenges the people to hearken in return. We could translate the biblical language quite colloquially: "Listen up! Pay attention!"

In any good relationship, each party has to attend to the other. The relationship works because this happens—and only when this happens. Hearkening is mutual: the people ask God to listen to them; God asks them to listen in return. Abraham's bargaining with

God over the fate of Sodom is a great example of mutual hearkening. The Lord determined to destroy the city, and Abraham challenged him: "Will you indeed sweep away the righteous with the wicked?" (Genesis 18:23). Abraham got God's attention. He appealed to divine justice—and proceeded to bargain down. If there were fifty righteous citizens, Abraham secured God's promise not to destroy the city. Then Abraham appealed for forty-five righteous citizens, then forty, thirty: Abraham pressed his luck to the limit. The presence of ten righteous people would spare the city. The bargaining happened only because Abraham made a claim on God's attention. God listened. Each party attended to the other.

Many people approach prayer as a bargain: "If you'll just let me pass this test or get that new job, I promise I'll . . ." A number of holy men and women owe their conversion to divine negotiation. Saint Francis of Assisi suddenly heard words Jesus spoke to a rich young man in search of eternal life as if they were addressed directly to him: "Go, sell what you own, and give the money to the poor, and you will have treasure in heaven; then come and follow me" (Mark 10:21). He gave away his considerable wealth. Fearing for his life in a violent thunderstorm, Martin Luther called on the protection of Saint Anne and promised to become a monk if he survived. Are these conversions genuine? Shall we dismiss them as crass exchanges? I think not. There's a grain of truth in divine negotiation. It is possible only because there is Someone with whom to bargain, Someone to call on in time of need. Someone will answer on the other end because Someone is paying attention. The stories suggest that prayer is a practice of mutual attending: we attend to God and allow God to attend to us.

I asked a good friend how her prayer life was, and she confessed that the twenty minutes she spent in silent prayer every morning before the day began had hit a dry spell. "Sometimes I fall asleep, so I take great comfort in the words of the psalmist, 'The Lord protects his children even as they sleep.'" Then she added, only half-joking: "I continue to show up. I'm afraid if I don't, something amazing might happen and I would have missed it!" She knows something important about relationships: they require some tending, even when the rewards are not obvious.

Over time attending to God becomes such a matter of habit that we are hardly aware of it as "prayer." Many years ago I posed the disciples' question to a wise spiritual director: "Teach me to pray." His response surprised me. I had expected a speech on the mechanics of praying, but he came back with questions. During the course of the day, when did I find myself talking to God? What spaces or places evoked the presence of the divine? When and where did I pause, focus, and attend to God's spirit of blessing? He invited me to think of those times and places as "prayer," even if I didn't consciously begin with God's name or conclude with the word *amen*. These were spaces of prayer.

I have passed on the invitation of this spiritual director to other groups of disciples and come up with a rich variety of "prayers." A man always stopped in his darkened garage for a moment of quiet before entering a house full of light and the bustle of children. A woman sat down at her kitchen table with a cup of coffee every morning for a few minutes after everyone else had gone to work and school. A business executive routinely paused before a window looking out onto the garden to collect her thoughts before heading in to chair a crucial meeting. A grandmother made certain to stand back and admire a fresh-scrubbed floor, a folded basket of laundry, a weeded garden. "I'm not just admiring my handiwork," she twinkled, "but I want to remind myself how good it is to have work and to be able to do it." These are the times and spaces of prayer. Sometimes we deliberately reach out to invoke the mysterious God "in whom we live and move and have our being" (Acts 17:28). At other times, that mystery reaches out to us, sometimes when we least expect it.

## Nurturing the Faith of a Child

Relationships change, and the relationship to which prayer attends is no exception. The apostle Paul recalled his childhood: "When I was a child, I spoke like a child, I thought like a child, I reasoned like a child, but when I became an adult, I put an end to childish ways" (1 Corinthians 13:11). He describes to the reader a child's-eye view of God. He prayed to this child's God, and maybe it was a white-bearded old man—or in Paul's case, a white-bearded old rabbi. Possibly Paul's childhood God was beyond human form entirely, like the God who spoke to Moses from a burning bush. But things changed. Paul himself changed dramatically on the road to Damascus, and his image of God changed dramatically as well. Whoever God was to him as a child, Paul now saw that God through the lens of "Jesus Christ, and him crucified" (1 Corinthians 2:2). That vision on the road forever altered his relationship with God, and he now saw with the eyes of an adult. Paul celebrated that transformation at the beginning and ending of every letter to every one of the churches under his care.

A lot of people have left the churches of their childhood and the gods of their youth. When asked why, they offer all kinds of reasons: "I don't believe in such a punishing God." "I hate thinking of God as a old man with a beard." "I felt like I was being judged all the time, and I got tired of worshiping a big old Judge on his Judgment Seat." Some told stories of the church's painful rejection of their gifts as women; others related tales of discrimination due to sexual orientation or background. Still others found church joyless and just plain boring. They all left as children or teenagers and never came back. Clearly, churches have a lot of apologies to make. But when people leave the church as children, their faith arrests at that age as well. They retain into adulthood images of God that are snapshots from a child's-eye view. These images cannot satisfy adult needs and adult wants. Had these people been permitted to grow into the faith the way someone would grow into any relationship, they would have discovered that the God to whom they pray has many different dimensions.

Discipleship is a journey. As we travel the road, we notice different things along the way. Perhaps we take in more of the countryside and less of the conversation around us. We attend to things differently. Iris Murdoch serves as one of my conversation partners along the way, though she would not have regarded herself as a Christian. Nonetheless, she makes an important observation that has stuck with me. Courage, she muses, is different to someone at twenty years of age than it is to someone at sixty. A virtue that the twenty-year-old defines largely in terms of physical fearlessness takes on the added dimensions of integrity with age. We would still call the virtue courage, but it's certainly more nuanced and complex. The same nuancing happens in our relationship with God. A quality of judgment shows itself to be shot through with mercy. An old man with a beard displays remarkably feminine qualities. The God we will know at the end of our lives is quite different from the God we knew at the beginning. We have changed—and God has changed us. A relationship matures and deepens.

A priest in spiritual direction was told by his director to imagine God as a woman—not just any woman or Woman in the abstract but the particular women whom he had loved. Initially the man was stunned, and he struggled with the director's guidance. But in time he gave in and summoned to his prayer the faces of his mother, his sisters, a colorful aunt, two women in a prayer group, a woman he'd almost left the priesthood to marry. Gradually he realized that God was loving him through the love of these women. They offered him concrete expressions of God's love, incarnating that love in particular ways. As the faces of these loving women haunted his prayer, he had to admit the sheer persistence of divine love. His relationship to God deepened as he began to contemplate the feminine face of God.

Relationships change; they ebb and flow. Sometimes they deepen and expand, like the priest's relationship with a God he discovered in the faces of the women he loved. But sometimes relationships enter what Saint John of the Cross spoke of as "the dark night of the soul." When prayer is dry and God seems absent, the ardent disciple feels abandoned, even as Jesus did on the cross. He could not even address God as "Father," and his cry of abandonment haunts us even today: "My God, my God, why have you forsaken me?" (Mark 15:34; Matthew 27:46). These were not Jesus' own words; he repeated the cry of anguish from Psalm 22. He could find no words of his own to speak—nor did he need to. The psalmist expressed it *for* him; the psalmist experienced it *before* him. Jesus' cry of anguish stands ready for us. When we encounter suffering too great to bear, we can utter the cry of Jesus.

Simone Weil returns again and again to Jesus' cry of abandonment. As a nurse in the Spanish Civil War and as a Jew in Vichy France, she knew hatred, discrimination, and suffering. She understood all too well how someone could feel abandoned by God. "Men struck down by affliction are at the foot of the Cross, almost at the greatest possible distance from God," she wrote.[2] Weil took great comfort in knowing that the dying Christ felt himself at an infinite remove from the God he once addressed as "Father." Weil felt that all human suffering fell somewhere in between the abyss of abandonment created between God the Father and God the crucified Son. Whatever suffering we experience, Jesus had already been there. He cried out in pain so that we would have words to use when we are lost, abandoned, and in anguish.

Martin Luther confronted such anguish in the faces of parents whose children had died in childbirth. They came to him in wordless despair, filled with grief and terrified that their unbaptized children would be consigned to eternal damnation. He urged the mothers to weep, to give way to those "sighs too deep for words" (Romans 8:26). He promised the parents that God would hear their wordless prayers and accept their tears as baptism for the infants.[3]

The Bible gives disciples prayers for times of anguish, prayers for times of abandonment, even prayers for sorrows that stretch beyond words. There is comfort in knowing that others have been there before us; there is grace is knowing Christ has already been to that darkest of places. Our relationship to God changes as we proceed on our journey of discipleship. Because the relationship changes, prayer changes as well. A good friend and longtime Jesuit describes his own changing relationship with God in prayer: "When I first started praying," he recalls," I talked *at* God, like you would talk at a stranger sitting next to you on a plane. Then, as the relationship deepened, I found myself talking *to* God, and then I spoke *with* God, as with a trusted friend." He paused and smiled at the memory. "Now," he continued, "I find myself *listening* to God. And more often than not, I am listening *for* God." Anyone who's been in a relationship of long standing understands this without explanation. Over time, every intimate relationship ranges between silence and speech. This happens in our relationship with God. Prayer is one of the spaces the relationship with God inhabits. Because the relationship with God is at once so important and so intimate, we join the disciples' plea: "Teach us how to pray."

## A Pattern for Prayer

Jesus responded to the disciples' plea with the Lord's Prayer. As Dietrich Bonhoeffer puts it, "Jesus told his disciples not only *how* they should pray but *what* they should pray. The Lord's Prayer is the essence of prayer."[4] Following Jesus' command, disciples pray the Lord's Prayer when they gather together and when they pray alone.

The Lord's Prayer patterns all other prayer. It constitutes a drama in three acts: we name God; we praise God; we petition God. The structure of the Lord's Prayer etches this pattern on our hearts. First, God is named—and named as "Our Father." Then that name is praised: "Hallowed be thy name." Praise broadens to embrace God's will and God's kingdom: "Thy kingdom come, thy will be done." The scope of this praise extends into the heavens and throughout the earth. Finally, specific petitions follow this encompassing praise: "Give us . . . ; forgive us . . . ; lead us . . . ; deliver us." Naming, praising, petitioning: these three acts loosely follow an ancient structure of liturgical prayer. This structure offers a flexible format for individual prayer.

## Naming God

Most Christian worship services begin by invoking the name of God. "In the name of the Father and of the Son and of the Holy Spirit," the pastor or priest intones. The congregation replies, "Amen." These words begin the worship service; they recur throughout the liturgy: the beginning of the eucharistic prayer, the conclusion of worship, various parts in between. What's in a name, and why do we keep repeating it? Are attention spans so short and distractions so great that worshipers would forget?

Christians gather in a *name*. They gather not just in any name but in the name of the Triune God—Father, Son, and Holy Spirit. In doing so, Christians name this God as their God. There are lots of other candidates waiting to claim our loyalties: self, money, family, success, wealth, fame, a particular grudge or cause. "That to which your heart clings and entrusts itself is, I say, really your God."[5] Like a licked stamp waiting for an envelope, our hearts attach themselves to all manner of unlikely gods.

Worship draws us back again and again to the name in which we gather, because we need reminding and we need reinforcing. The liturgy does not advance in a straight line; rather it circles back again and again to the name of the God in whom we gather. We worship in this name; we assemble before this God.

As we identify our God as this God—Father, Son, and Spirit—we simultaneously identify ourselves. We are the kind of people who worship this kind of God. Naming tells us who God is, but it also tells us who we are. In naming ourselves as people of this kind of God, we acknowledge that this God has claimed us. We claim this God in return. All of this happens in prayer as we address the God to whom we pray. In worship we assemble and reassemble in the name of the Triune God.

Yet as we move through the liturgy, we circle back to address God in a variety of ways. Each of our prayers calls out to God in bold and direct address. From the storehouse of memory, we call to mind God's history with us. This is a God who not only *has* a distinctive history with the faithful; this is a God who *created* history and all its tools: time, memory, and the capacity to tell stories. Whether we name God as "King of the Universe" or "the Beginning and End of all things," each name telegraphs an ancient story.

Feminist Christians rightly underscore two problems with traditional masculine forms for addressing God. First, using masculine names for God has meant that women became second-class citizens in church life and practice. These injustices demand correction. Envisioning God as masculine truncates the mystery, and feminist Christians lobby for feminine nomenclature in worship and prayer. They point to the breadth of the biblical witness to God, names like "Wisdom," "Sophia," "Mother," and "Lover." In addition, the battles over inclusive language underscore the awkwardness of any human language in speaking of the divine. Here a Muslim proverb gives comfort: "There are a hundred names of God, of which humans know only ninety-nine. Only the camel knows the hundredth." No single word can ever capture the full picture—and who would want to get close enough to a camel to find out the hundredth name of God? No single gender and no androgynous combination of both can contain the mystery. All our titles merely point in the direction of what we now see "in a mirror dimly, but then we will see face to face" (1 Corinthians 13:12).

We have many names for God, and that is right and proper. If we think about the One to whom we pray in the course of the standard Sunday worship service, we reap a full harvest: "Father and Mother of us all," "Creator," "Blessed Trinity," "Lord," "Spirit of creation," "the Beginning and the End," "Shepherd of Israel." Add to these evocative names the addresses of hymns and songs scattered throughout the service, and we more than make up the ninety-nine names. Yet the sum of all these names adds up to less than the whole. God is greater than them all.

Moreover, these names are storied. Behind each name is a narrative, and in speaking the name, we remember the story that gave rise to it. We reenter that particular history. The Old Testament bears names like "King of the Universe," "I am Who I am," and the deliberately unpronounceable YHWH. These titles hold stories of majesty and wonder, mystery and reverence. Jesus introduced a new story—and a new title as well. He addressed this God as "Father." In doing so, he distilled all prior names of God into the intimate relationship between a father and his children.

Naming works both ways. In identifying God, we identify ourselves. In naming God as "Father," Jesus identified himself as God's Son. He invited his disciples to do the same, thereby identifying them as children of this God, as well as his own brothers and sisters. Accepting Jesus' invitation, we call on God as "Father" and name ourselves as his daughters and sons. We acknowledge that God cares for God's people as a loving father cares for his children.

Sometimes the relationship to God calls out other metaphors. Crying out to the Lord as "my rock, my fortress, and my deliverer, my God, my rock in whom I take refuge, my shield, and the horn of my salvation, my stronghold" (Psalms 18:2), the psalmist deployed military images in a bid for protection. Elsewhere the writer took the role of a vulnerable animal dependent on someone else for survival: "The Lord is my shepherd, I shall not want" (Psalms 23:1). The haunting words of Psalms 22 and 88 speak from the abyss of abandonment and plead for any signal that God cares:

> My God, my God, why have you forsaken me?
> Why are you so far from helping me,
> from the words of my groaning?
> O my God, I cry by day, but you do not answer;
> and by night, but find no rest [Psalms 22:1–2].

> But I, O Lord, cry out to you;
> In the morning my prayer comes before you.
> O Lord, why do you cast me off?
> Why do you hide your face from me? . . .
> You have caused friend and neighbor to shun me;
> my companions are in darkness [Psalms 88:13–14, 18].

The psalms play out a full spectrum of emotions and a wide range of relationships between God and God's creatures. The psalmist offered prayer to God, and as he prayed, he identified himself in relationship to a certain dimension of the divine. If God was a shepherd, he rested in the security of that shepherd's flock. If God was a fortress, he stood protected within. If God's face was turned away, he protested with all the bitterness and outrage of a spurned lover. Because of the range of relationships catalogued in the psalms, many spiritual directors invite their directees simply to pray through the psalter. They familiarize themselves with the many names of God. In identifying God differently, disciples reposition themselves in different ways before the divine, assuming roles they might not otherwise have been able to imagine.

A doctor describes the consolation one patient found in the dark verses of Psalm 88. The psalmist had been abandoned by his friends, his lovers—even by God, and the psalm concludes in despair: "Darkness is my only companion." Centuries later, a patient with a terminal illness found comfort in the fact that someone else had shared the space of his despair and put it into words. The psalms remain a powerful storehouse of names for God and metaphors for the spectrum of relationships God has with humans.

Then there is the God who is utterly beyond our attempts at description. God spoke to Job from the whirlwind, and the words assault all claims to familiarity with a barrage of images:

> Where were you when I laid the
> foundation of the earth?
> Tell me, if you have understanding.
> Who determined its measurements—surely you know!
> Or who stretched the line upon it?
> On what were its bases sunk or who laid its cornerstone,
> when the morning stars sang together,
> and all the heavenly beings shouted for joy? [Job 38:4–7].

Job responded by collapsing into wonder: "Therefore I have uttered what I did not understand, things too wonderful for me, which I did not know. . . . I had heard of you by the hearing of the ear, but now my eye sees you" (Job 42:3, 5). Then Job lapsed into silence. Such a God was beyond language. In words or in silence, prayer names the God to whom we pray. At the same time, we identify ourselves as worshipers of this kind of God, a process of mutual naming.

## Praising God

Most liturgical churches use an opening prayer or collect in their services. I have always loved these prayers because they tell people why they are there. More important, they tell people whom they worship. Collects are vehicles of pure praise. In the book of worship for my own communion, a collect for the Festival of the Transfiguration reads like this: "O God, in the transfiguration of your Son you confirmed the mysteries of the faith by the witness of Moses and Elijah, and in the voice from the bright cloud you foreshadowed our adoption as your children. Make us with the king heirs of your glory, and bring us to enjoy its fullness, through Jesus Christ our Lord, who lives and reigns with you and the Holy Spirit, one God, now and forever. Amen." Like most opening prayers, this one features a long descriptive section: "you confirmed the mysteries of the faith," "you foreshadowed our adoption." In simple past tense, the collect recounts the story of the transfiguration. On the feast day itself, this story is proclaimed in the Gospel reading, but here it is condensed into a prayer. Why? Is there some need to remind God of the liturgical calendar? Are we afraid God will forget what happened? Are we afraid the congregation will lose track of the significance of this festival day between the beginning of worship and the reading of the Gospel? What's going on?

The Gospel reading tells the story of the transfiguration; the prayer opens it for our participation. No longer spectators, we enter the story. Prayer places us with Peter and the other disciples on our knees and open-mouthed in wonder. The language of prayer makes present the past. Instead of speaking *about* God, we speak *to* God: "*You* did this; *you* did that."

Prayer depends on direct address; it is conversation with God. When anything important is about to happen in the Old Testament, the language shifts to direct address. Events are no longer narrated, as in "David again gathered all the chosen men of Israel, thirty thousand" (2 Samuel 6:1). When something important happens, the action unfolds right before our eyes. "But that same night the word of the Lord came to Nathan, 'Go and tell my servant David'" (2 Samuel 7:4–5). The words "But God said . . ." signal that fireworks are about to begin. So it is in prayer.

When we pray, we address God directly. We call out to the mystery and place ourselves in its presence. Everyone can put the story of the transfiguration in their own words: "Jesus sent up to a mountain to pray, and Moses and Elijah appeared to him. Then Peter wanted to build booths" and so on. The story narrates the event; with prayer we enter it. We address God as "you, the one who confirmed Jesus' kingship" from within the event itself. Prayer closes the gap in time and space between the event reported and its ongoing effects. When we enter the transfiguration, praise falls from our lips. We speak from direct experience of the wondrous things God has done. We do not stand in God's debt; we stand in God's presence. That is gracious space indeed.

Prayer remembers. In language that itself seems divine, the ancient prayers of the liturgy recall God's history with the creation. We repeat these prayers not because we fear forgetting the events they remember but because we want to remind ourselves, literally, to re-mind ourselves. Think of how often parents tell their children to "Mind me!" More is going on than a simple command to "Do what I tell you to do." Minding someone means aligning oneself with someone who wants what is best for us.

In his letter to the Philippians, the apostle Paul tells the community to "Mind Christ!" He places a popular Christological hymn in the body of his letter:

[Christ Jesus], who, though he was in the form of God,
did not count equality with God as something to be
exploited,
but emptied himself, taking the form of a slave
[Philippians 2:5–11].

The hymn is almost as familiar to Christians today as it would have been to Paul's audience. What we miss is Paul's preface. In effect, Paul told his beloved Philippian congregation to mind someone, to align themselves with the Christ described in the hymn: "Have this in mind among yourselves which is yours in Christ Jesus." In praying the hymn, Paul invited his congregation to enter the cosmic story of a heavenly redeemer who came to earth and walked among people, then died and was raised by God in glory. Paul hoped they would not only recite the story but enter it. When they truly "have this story in mind," they would live as if Christ still walked among them. "Be on the lookout!" Paul implied. "Christ is in your midst!"

Praise works the same way, whether we offer it from a pew or in private. We address God directly. Reminding ourselves of the many graces in our lives, we admit that despite all evidence to the contrary, God walks among us and we walk with God. Praise witnesses to the divine presence in our midst, claiming the stuff of our lives as somehow touched by the divine.

A friend related the story of her husband's sudden surgery at a hospital far from their home. She found herself in a waiting room filled with anxious strangers, all awaiting word from the surgeons. She remembered trying to pray: "I couldn't think clearly enough to come up with words, and all of my usual warm-up prayers seemed somehow trivial. I found myself saying the words of the great Trisagion, 'Holy God, Holy and Mighty, Holy and Immortal,' over and over and over again. As I prayed, I was overcome by a feeling of gratitude that utterly surprised me. Here I was in a strange place and someone I loved was having serious surgery. I was anxious, and everyone around me was worried too. I still don't understand it, but the prayer swept me into this great goodness, and I felt at peace." The words of this ancient prayer—literally, praise of God as thrice-blessed—left the woman awash in thanksgiving.

Praise and gratitude reinforce one another. One expresses thanks for a gift given and moves without hesitation to praise the giver. This happens in great ways and small. A beloved uncle gives his nephew a much coveted train set, and the child's delight in the gift prompts praise of the giver. "Uncle Adam, you always know just what I want!" the child squeals in delight. A nonprofit organization thanks a generous benefactor for her gift. Gratitude spills over into praise for the giver's generosity. A lover expresses thanks for a surprise Valentine's Day dinner and moves effortlessly into praise of the one before her eyes. A retirement honors a faithful employee, and the evening of festivities gratefully recounts the things he has done and the person he has been. Gratitude is intimately bound up with praise.

Prayer displays the interdependence between praise and gratitude. For the woman at the hospital, praise prompted gratitude. As she blessed the person of the Triune God, gratitude overwhelmed her for the Giver of all gifts. At other times, gratitude gives way to praise. A child delighted with the gift of a new train set turned to praise the giver. Gratitude for a gift becomes praise for the giver; praise of the giver calls to mind the gifts given. But sometimes we are in need and must ask for something we lack. We come to the third movement in prayer: petition.

## Petitioning God

Asking for something we need sounds simple enough. We are used to stating what we want, everything from a piece of cake to a person's absolute attention. It's a game of "gimme," whether our wants are trivial or profoundly important. "Give me a new car." "Give us a peaceful and just world." "Give us a stable economy." Look at the

petitions in the Lord's Prayer, the prayer Jesus offers as the model
for Christian prayer:

> Give us this day our daily bread.
> And forgive us our debts, as we also have forgiven our
> debtors.
> And do not bring us to the time of trial,
> but rescue us from the evil one [Matthew 6:11–13].

"Give us . . . , forgive us . . . , do not bring us . . . , rescue us."
Prayer simply transfers the "gimme" game onto God—or does it?
What is petition all about?

## Discerning Wants and Needs

In his teaching and preaching, Jesus spoke a lot about asking for
what we need. This alone suggests that petition is neither straight-
forward nor easy. One of the things that makes petition hard is the
difference between wants and needs. Actress Judi Dench relates a
story about her doting father and a pair of expensive blue-and-white
shoes she saw on holiday in Spain.[6] She wanted those shoes with
all the yearning of a fifteen-year-old fashion-conscious girl. Her
father surveyed them gravely and then suggested that they consider
the purchase over lunch. At a seafood buffet, the girl's eyes were distracted by four huge prawns, which she devoured with delight. At
the end of the meal, her father observed, "You've just eaten your
shoes." Our wants take us everywhere: now to a pair of shoes, now
to a meal of prawns, now to a cause or longed-for opportunity.

The problem with wants is that they often mask our deepest
needs. Dench relates the story in her sixties. The shoes she so
wanted are long forgotten. She may not have gotten everything
she wanted at the time, but she certainly had what she needed: the
love only a father could give her. The shoes, even the prawns, were
an ephemeral longing. Anyone in recovery knows the difference

between wants and needs. What an addict wants is another drink or fix; what an addict needs is sobriety, liberation from addiction. A recovering cocaine addict who supported his habit through theft talked about sobriety: "Eleven years later I can still spot the perfect robbery. That's who we are. No matter where we are these thoughts will drag us down. And the only people who will understand is us."[7] Addicts need a new center of gravity for their lives, a center that can hold. A woman, clean and sober for fourteen years, said, "There's this God-shaped hole in me that I kept pouring booze into. When I stopped drinking, I had to deal with that."

Dealing with that basic need for God reorients our wants and desires. It's not that we should ignore them—or pretend that they don't exist. In a world according to God, we pray for what we need, and God is what we need to reorient and reframe all our wants. Jesus invites disciples to pray for concrete things: food, forgiveness, freedom from fear. The invitation points them to an important truth about the God to whom he prays: this God worries about what we need to flourish, and this God loves us in the concrete.

Looking for a new angle on Valentine's Day, a group of parents asked their children about love. What did love mean to them? Their answers were all very concrete. "When Mommy makes Daddy a pot of coffee and tastes a cup before giving it to him. That's love." "When my puppy licks me before I go to bed. And I haven't played with him that day at all." "Grandma got arthritis and couldn't bend over to paint her toenails any more. So Grandpa did it—even after he got arthritis." There are no grand theories here; these children found love incarnate in the particular. Details captured and displayed it. So it is with God. God counts on the details to express love. Jesus encourages his disciples to ask for the basic stuff of daily life.

Having asked for "our daily bread," we know whom to thank when we receive it. We thank the one whom we asked for food. Receiving the gifts we asked for points us again to the giver of all good gifts. My husband and his siblings stood by helplessly as their mother slid further and further into Alzheimer's. They realized she would no longer be safe in the family home. Members of the family did all their homework, visiting and checking out various nursing homes and care facilities. They also prayed and asked God for what they needed: a room in a good facility. When a place opened up at one of their top choices, the eldest son declared it as a "godsend," quite literally, a gift from God. Because the family had asked for divine assistance, they were grateful when it arrived. Because they had asked for God's help, they knew whom to thank. Perhaps that's the divine intention in petition: creating people of gratitude. In asking and receiving, people gradually begin to see their lives as blessed, and they turn to thank the source of all blessing.

## The Countercultural Value of Dependence

Throughout the Gospels, Jesus invited the disciples to "ask and it will be given you" (Matthew 7:7; Luke 11:9). Jesus suspected that people have a hard time distinguishing between wants and needs. But he also challenged their desire for independence. The disciples found it hard to be in need. Asking for what they needed was no more welcome to them than it is to us. Asking for what we need does not come naturally. Why is asking for help so unnatural? What is so hard about asking for what we need?

Part of the problem is that we're used to *having* everything we need. We value independence; we revere people who seem to "have it all"; we worship independence. If you doubt any of this, try taking a driver's license away from an elderly relative who drives too dangerously to be on the road. Now she will have to ask to be taken everywhere. The burden of her dependence falls both on her and on those who will have to chauffeur her around. Yet independence is not what God has in mind for her—or for any of us. As much as we'd like to be "our own persons," we belong to someone else. As the apostle Paul reminds us, "You belong to Christ, and Christ belongs to God" (1 Corinthians 3:23). Having and belonging operate in different solar systems.

A familiar offertory prayer puts this directly: "Merciful Father, we offer with joy and thanksgiving, what you have first given us: our selves, our time, and our possessions, signs of your gracious love." A focus on having would put "our selves, our time, and our possessions" at the center, and our lives would revolve around them. Over time, we would become possessed by our possessions, like the rich fool in the parable who was too successful for his own good (Luke 12:13–21). He built larger and larger barns to store all his extra grain, and the huge towers reached into the sky, shrines to the farmer's success. The towers organized the rich man's life—until quite suddenly he died. The parable may point to the follies of excess, but I've always regarded it as a simple exorcism. Death finally frees the rich man to belong to Christ once again, rather than being possessed by his possessions.

A more modern parable from the African jungle speaks of liberation and enslavement. A species of small, delicate monkeys swing freely among the trees. They are highly prized by zoos all over the world but difficult to capture without harm. Clever trappers realized they could appeal to the monkeys' greed. They hollowed out gourds, filled them with peanuts, and placed small holes the size of a monkey's hand in the sides. The trappers hung the gourds in the trees and waited. Attracted by food, the monkeys reached in and grabbed great handfuls of peanuts. Then they discovered they were unable to withdraw the handfuls of peanuts through the tiny holes. The trappers easily bagged them. The trappers knew something the monkeys didn't. They knew that the monkeys would refuse to release their peanuts, even under threat of capture. If they would only let go, they could swing free through the jungle. But they hang desperately on to those nuts.

God worries that humans have not advanced much beyond their primate cousins. Petition is God's way of teaching disciples to unclench their hands. We are created to move through life with open hands. The inheritance from Grandpa Ryan, the refund from the IRS, the paycheck that rolls in every two weeks—are these entitlements? earnings? gifts? How can we receive with open hands? How can we ask for what we need?

On his deathbed, Martin Luther remarked that we are all beggars. It was an odd remark for the dying man to make, but Luther wanted to leave his family and friends with the image of open hands. This was the way to "belong to Christ." We move through life with hand outstretched and open for the hand of the neighbor. In a world according to God, asking for what we need is the antidote to the consuming desire to have—and to have more. It is God's way of freeing us from our possessions and freeing us for the wonder of creation.

# 6

Forgiveness

*Healing and Being Healed*

Prodded by his disciples to be introduced to the God whom he addressed as "Father," Jesus responded with the Lord's Prayer. This simple prayer covers the basics. After praising God and praying for the coming of God's kingdom on earth, the prayer petitions God for what Christians most need in the journey of discipleship. People need food, clothing, and shelter, the three things essential to human survival. To be disciples, however, people need food, protection, and forgiveness, the three things requested in the Lord's Prayer. Forgiveness ranks alongside the need for food and protection as something essential to Christian discipleship. Why?

Without forgiveness, the disciples risk killing themselves and others in a cycle of unending violence. Forgiveness enables the disciples to steer a middle course between self-hatred and hatred of others, between self-destruction and annihilation of everyone else. Without forgiveness, disciples would travel alone, alienated from others by slights and petty grievances. A single petition charts a course of reconciliation for every disciple: "Forgive us our trespasses, as we forgive those who trespass against us."

These are not easy words to speak, and daily repetition does not make them any easier. Forgiveness is an unnatural act because every natural reflex strains toward retaliation, alienation, and payback. It is an impossible demand, literally beyond human capacity. The good news is that this impossible demand is also a divine gift. Jesus urges disciples to pray daily for the ability to forgive, reminding them that they too stand in need of forgiveness. Forgiveness may be contrary to the human spirit; however, it is the essence of the divine spirit. As they experience the grace of divine forgiveness, Jesus hopes that disciples will find it easier to forgive those who have wronged them. He wants us to become practiced in the art of forgiveness. As we forgive and experience forgiveness, we will become forgiven forgivers.

This does not happen overnight; indeed, it is a miracle of grace that forgiveness happens at all. Forgiveness inches forward through steps of repenting, remembering, and reconciling. The first step in forgiveness enables disciples to turn away from violence. As we pray, "Forgive us our trespasses . . . ," we remind ourselves that we too are sinners in need of repentance. No matter how unjust our suffering, we yearn to return evil for evil. Repenting of own capacity for violence, we refuse retaliation and embrace forgiveness instead. Repentance is the first step in forgiveness—and revenge is its chief temptation.

The second step in forgiveness overturns the popular counsel to "forgive and forget." Forgetting the unjust injury often only fuels passive aggression and denial. Memory freshens an injury, but it also underscores a daily need to turn consciously away from avenging it. In remembering our own tendency toward revenge and our own desperate need for repentance, we open ourselves to be re-membered in the body of Christ. Remembering is the second step in forgiveness— and amnesia is its chief temptation.

Reconciliation is the final step in forgiveness, enabling disciples to embrace Jesus' most difficult command: "Love your enemies; pray for those who persecute you" (Matthew 5:44). Recrimination blocks reconciliation, for it refuses solidarity and chooses alienation. These steps make up the process of forgiveness: repenting, remembering, and reconciling.

It would be easy to think that in mastering these steps, disciples have learned to walk. That would be wishful thinking indeed. Mastery of these three steps, no matter how many times we take them, comes slowly, if at all. We stumble along the journey of discipleship. In our inability to forgive, we are the halt, the lame, and the blind, ever in search of a miracle. For that reason, we pray for grace, petitioning daily: "Forgive us our trespasses, as we forgive those who trespass against us." We wait for the miracle that is forgiveness.

## "Forgive Us Our Trespasses": Repenting

Daily reminders of the need for forgiveness are not welcome. Everyone clamors for the status of being an innocent victim, sinless and without blemish. As any parent summoned to settle a fight between two young children knows, it is never that simple. Despite teary protestations of innocence, evidence of provocation abounds. "I didn't do a thing!" often translates into "I pushed her just a little— and then she hit me!" The petition for forgiveness in the Lord's Prayer does not care "whodunit"; it settles neither blame nor fault. It simply positions people for repentance: "Forgive us." Those who pray this prayer shed their presumptive innocence, reminding themselves again and again that Christ is the only "innocent victim." The petition presents repentance as the first move in the practice of forgiveness.

Repentance and forgiveness together break the cycle of violence that revenge releases. In his thoughtful book *Exclusion and Embrace*, Miroslav Volf tells the story of a Muslim schoolteacher from the former Yugoslavia who taught literature in the village school. Through literature, she taught her students about beauty and love. As war spread through the country, she was beaten and violated by Serbs in her village whom she had known as colleagues, neighbors, and students. Reeling from the brutalization, she named her newborn son Jihad. The first time she raised the child to her breast, she said, "May this milk choke you if you forget."[1] These events unleash a spiral of revenge. A young boy named Jihad learns to hate. Jihad teaches his children to hate, his children teach their children to hate, and the inheritance of generations is violence. Words from the Old Testament seem less like a curse than the hopeless description of life in a world that does not live according to God. Children are punished "for the iniquity of their parents, to the third and the fourth generation of those who reject me" (Exodus 20:5).

How many stories of revenge illustrate the cumulative effect of violence? I steal a lamb from your fold; you respond by burning down my farm; I retaliate by murdering your children; the neighbors take sides; a village is at war. Retaliation exceeds the originating offense, and it becomes hard to remember what started the whole cascade of violence in the first place—and by that time no one wants to remember. The violence has become an end in itself.

Against the specter of escalating violence, ancient codes of law cautioned moderation: "An eye for an eye, a tooth for a tooth." What sounds like a brutal arithmetic of vengeance actually counsels limit: "Just *one* eye for an eye; just *one* tooth for a tooth." I know that if someone were to pluck out my eye, I would shout, "Off with your head!" Natural instinct reacts to offense with overwhelming force. The juggernaut of violence lurches forward.

What stops revenge in its tracks? Repentance puts up the first road block in this bloody path. Repentance confesses the natural impulse toward revenge—and then steps back from it. When every cell in one's body screams for retaliation, repentance admits the desire for revenge: "I want to do to you what you have done to me—but I choose not to. I want to hurt you—but I turn away from violence."

Too often people treat forgiveness and repentance as if they were separate job descriptions: one for the victim, the other for the perpetrator. The perpetrator's task is to repent; the victim's, to forgive. This kind of casuistry scuttles any possibility for authentic forgiveness, opening the door for endless calculation. Should repentance precede forgiveness? How much repentance is enough? How long should one repent, so you know he is really, really sorry? Is the repentance sincere? Is the forgiveness genuine? Should there be additional recompense? If so, how much? Whatever forgiveness comes of such debate is its own form of vengeance in disguise.

The forgiveness Jesus calls for—forgiven forgiveness—begins with the startling demand for repentance from everyone, *including the victim*, as the victim both acknowledges the desire for revenge and renounces it. In addition, repentance on the part of the victim short-circuits the temptation to make generalized judgments, assessing a group of people on the basis of an injury from one person. Injury often fuels stereotyping: "All men are like that!" "What can you expect from a Republican!" "Gay men can't be role models." Prejudice and stereotyping magnify the impact of a single offense, mitigating the effect of any pardon and lingering to poison the attitudes of others. Repentance on the part of the victim is the first movement in the practice of forgiveness.

Repentance resists an almost irresistible desire to return evil for evil. Repentance invites everyone to confess the dark side of the Golden Rule: "I could do unto you what you have done unto me. I could hurt you as you have hurt me—and worse. I could hurt you and your family and your loved ones. I could do all of this—and I want to." Repentance confesses all of this.

Repentance on the part of the victim displays a miracle of grace. In praying to "Forgive us our trespasses, as we forgive those who trespass against us," a victim confesses noninnocence. Confessing an inclination to retaliate may be the first miracle of repentance. In telling her story, the Muslim schoolteacher may be making a small gesture of repentance. She has to listen to herself describe the difference between who she was and who she has become. Someone who taught love and literature now instructs her own children in revenge. The interview itself could signal a miracle of repentance.

Such miracles happen all the time, often unnoticed. Forgiveness may be "unnatural," but grace softens hearts hardened by hurt. "I gave as good as I got!" one of my aunts used to boast wickedly at a family gathering, and the assembled relatives would all laugh. Her long, rich life took a lot of rough turns. I detected in the boast a trace of wistfulness and wondered if she wished she could have figured out how to give a little less in return. Her brash words counted as a tiny miracle of repentance. She'd been no angel, and her very boast expressed a kind of solidarity with the offender. We are all wrapped up in the messiness of being human, tempted toward revenge and contemplating payback.

"Forgive us . . . as we forgive." Daily repetition of this prayer reminds the faithful that repentance is the posture of disciples, whatever the wrongs they suffer. This need not happen in front of the offender, a move that might only encourage bad behavior or blunt the sharpness of the offense. The Lord's Prayer describes confession *before God*, the source of all mercy. Discipleship does not confer innocence; rather, disciples rejoice in the fact that they follow the one who was innocence incarnate, Jesus Christ, the only innocent victim.

Repentance stands as the first movement in forgiveness. It needs to precede forgiveness so that forgiveness can be more than a nonviolent form of revenge. Fast-forwarding to forgiveness can derail the process of reconciliation, which may be painful but necessary. For example, a friend "forgave" her husband's infidelity but proceeded to make him pay for it in great ways and small. She withheld affection; she grew bitter and resentful; she etched their marriage with the acid of jealousy. Had she confessed her own desire for revenge outright, they might have been able to work toward reconciliation. Instead, she moved too quickly to a strained forgiveness, which entrapped both parties in a web of resentment.

Repentance paves the way for authentic forgiveness. Repenting the desire to retaliate, forgiveness refuses to respond in kind. Forgiveness resists throwing any fuel on the fire whatever, and without more to burn, the fire extinguishes itself. Philosopher Hannah Arendt addresses the need for forgiveness in a world bent on revenge. A deed stimulates reactions that escalate in both intensity and violence, and "we would remain the victims of its consequences forever, not unlike the sorcerer's apprentice who lacked the magic formula to break the spell."[2] Forgiveness alone breaks the cycle of violence. Repentance is its first movement.

## "As We Forgive Those Who Trespass Against Us": Remembering

As a practice of discipleship, forgiveness renounces the pious aphorism: "Forgive and forget." The Christian practice of forgiveness is not about forgetting but about remembering. Forgiveness creates a dangerous memory because it permits truthful recollection of the past without the danger of reinjury or the revival of fresh rage. In the aftermath of apartheid in South Africa, the Truth and Reconciliation Commission chose not to issue broad amnesty to wrongdoers on both sides of the conflict, wiping the slate clean. Instead, the commission opted to create a space where citizens could remember. Both victims and offenders needed to say what they had seen and done. Only when people truthfully faced the past could they move into a future filled with hope. A truthful account of past wrongs disables their power to enthrall the future.

Jesus' first disciples wrestled with painful memories of their own faithlessness and Jesus' incomparable mercy. They remembered Judas in the Garden of Gethsemane, betraying Jesus to the temple guards with a kiss. Betrayal is the fatal sin in friendship, and Jesus held Judas accountable for the deed with words that haunted him for the rest of his brief life: "Friend, do what you are here to do" (Matthew 26:50). Nor was Judas the only disciple to betray his Lord. Later that evening in the courtyard of the high priest, Peter denied Jesus not once but three times. Then, on Golgotha, Jesus was crucified between two common criminals; the authorities could not find any of the disciples around him. They had scattered in fear. After the resurrection, the disciples went into hiding. They were probably just as terrified of running into Jesus, the man whom they had betrayed. When the disciples locked themselves into an upper room, Jesus suddenly appeared among them, bearing forgiveness.

The words were so unexpected that Jesus had to repeat himself: "Peace be with you." With these words, he gave the disciples what they most needed but could not ask for: forgiveness. He forgave them a shocking string of betrayals; he offered them forgiveness.

Only after all of these painful encounters of forgiveness and reconciliation did the disciples receive their ministries of reconciliation. After he had remembered and forgiven their disloyalty, Jesus charged them to forgive others, even as they had been forgiven. He entrusted to these forgiven friends the practice of forgiveness. "If you forgive the sins of any, they are forgiven them; if you retain the sins of any, they are retained" (John 20:23). As the disciples moved out into the world, the memory of this painful history shaped ministries of compassion. They forgave others—and remembered their own need for forgiveness. They remembered their own fecklessness—and forgave others. Every encounter with a sinner seeking forgiveness reminded them of Jesus' own lavish mercy toward them. Every confession recalled their own gracious metamorphosis from betrayers to confessors. Every absolution the disciples offered repeated the words that had unburdened their guilty consciences: "Peace be with you." For the rest of their lives, the disciples were marked by the memory of their own profound need for forgiveness. In forgiving they would remember. In remembering they would forgive. Forgive—and remember. Remember—and forgive. Forgiveness and remembrance were fused together, and the disciples became forgiven forgivers.

Their story becomes our story. Each liturgical year we reenact the passion and resurrection of Jesus. We play the disciples, and as we move through the passion, we rehearse again our own profound need to be forgiven, and we forgive. We identify with their terrible confusion during the events of Holy Week, and we understand how we would do exactly the same. Then we hear words that Jesus speaks to us: "Peace be with you." The Lord's Prayer sums up our transformation in a single petition: "Forgive us our trespasses, as we forgive those who trespass against us."

Memory can be excruciating for a victim who is less than divine. For this reason, much of the therapeutic literature on forgiveness counsels amnesia. "Get on with your life!" "Start with a clean slate!" Self-help books and the slogans they promote offer forgiveness as a way of moving on. Experts argue that whenever victims remember an injury, they replay it. They rightly recognize that unless victims learn forgiveness, the hurts they receive return to reinjure them.

My colleague Ann recalled a betrayal that happened several years ago. As she spoke, her face colored, her voice trembled, and her pulse began to race. Even though the event was long past, it was as if it had happened yesterday. Time marked by calendars and clocks did not apply here. Like most victims, Ann relived the injury as she recounted it.

What role does memory serve in Ann's situation? Remembering merely replays a painful scenario, reviving all the negative emotions evoked in the first place. Yet forgetting a traumatic experience never works. A chance encounter, a turn of phrase, even a smell can bring the event back afresh, its power undiminished by time. Ann must cultivate a way of remembering that does not reinjure her.

Ann has a choice, and being clear about what her choice is can both empower her and move her toward healing. On the one hand, Ann can choose to remain a victim, secretly harboring the hurt and identifying herself as "victim." The injury then becomes a shrine she tends, treasures, and reverences daily. Over time, worship at this shrine will form her and deform her, because it now focuses her life. Ann remains in the thrall of resentment.

On the other hand, Ann can choose to move away from victimhood. She may get frustrated that someone else controls her life: "I realized this whole thing was renting too much space in my head," she may say. "I decided to renegotiate the rental agreement." She may get bored: "I just got tired of being a victim. I wanted things to change, and the only thing I could work on was me." Whatever the reasons, a former victim chooses to reclaim her life. She moves from a "me" posture, as in "you hurt *me*," into an "I" posture, as in "*I* want things to change." Turning consciously away from victimhood, she departs from a vicious cycle of reinjury. Ann may work deliberately to defuse the impact of the offense. Sometimes this involves a direct confrontation with the offender; sometimes the offender has died or moved away. Whatever course of action Ann follows, the offense she has suffered does not grip her. She can remember without reinjury. Therapeutically, forgiveness offers her a way of detaching and moving forward.

Forgiveness as a Christian practice pushes beyond therapy. A ministry of reconciliation is different from therapeutic detachment. Disciples remember the example of Jesus, who followed none of the therapeutic counsel in his own practice of forgiveness. Instead of moving forward, Jesus moved back. He returned to the scene of the betrayal and to the disciples who had abandoned him. Instead of detaching, Jesus returned to reattach and reconnect to the very friends who betrayed him. He returned to repair damage that was uniquely their own, and he returned in peace. In reconnecting with his friends, he neither ignored their offense nor pretended it away. He simply offered them peace. As forgiven forgivers, these disciples moved with Jesus into God's future. This is the role of reconciliation in a world according to God.

Forgiveness becomes a ministry of re-membering, literally, a reintegration of all things into the fullness from which they came. The author of Colossians suggests nothing less: "For in him all the fullness of God was pleased to dwell, and through him God was pleased to reconcile to himself all things, whether on earth or in heaven, by making peace through the blood of his cross" (Colossians 1:19–20). God works "to reconcile all things to himself" through the disciples' practice of forgiveness.

An Armenian woman escaped a concentration camp in World War II to become an army nurse. Later, in a camp for prisoners, she was assigned a badly wounded man who had served as a guard in the camp. As she nursed him back to health, he stopped her one day and said, "Your face looks familiar." "Yes," she said quietly, "I was one of your prisoners." "Why have you helped me?" he asked, incredulous. "Because I am a Christian," she replied. "We are taught to forgive." Reconciliation for this woman reached out to bring an offender back into the community of the living.

In the scope of cosmic reconciliation, the line between victim and offender blurs. Over a lifetime, disciples find they have played both roles with equal ease. The focus of biblical forgiveness is reconciliation. Two New Testament passages point to its importance in very different ways. The Gospel of Mark urges all victims to forgive: "Whenever you stand praying, forgive, if you have anything against anyone; so that your Father who is in heaven may also forgive you your trespasses"(Mark 11:25). The Gospel of Matthew repeats virtually the same saying, only applying it in his context to all offenders: "So when you are offering your gift at the altar, if you remember that your brother or sister has something against you, leave your gift there before the altar and go; first be reconciled to your brother or sister, and then come and offer your gift" (Matthew 5:23–24). Matthew's Gospel raises the bar. He demands reconciliation, whether the offense is real or imagined. The sole factor determining the need for reconciliation is whether someone "has something against you." Taken together, these two passages trace the scope of reconciliation. The journey of discipleship moves toward reconciliation of all victims and offenders into the body of Christ. God works in each to restore the creation to its intended fullness.

A legend about the disciple Judas illustrates the reach of divine reconciliation. The canonical biblical texts present Judas as a tragic example of the power of guilt. His deed brought him censure from his friends, ridicule from the Temple hierarchy, and overwhelming isolation. Alone and miserable, Judas watched events he set in motion spin out of his control. He could no longer live with himself. Crushed by the weight of his crime, Judas hanged himself in a potter's field. The biblical story ends in suicide, but an extracanonical legend keeps the cameras rolling. According to this legend,

Jesus descended into hell after his crucifixion. There he remembered Judas. Jesus sought him out among the lost souls in hell in order to unburden him. Jesus found Judas to remember—and to forgive.

## "Love Your Enemies; Pray for Those Who Persecute You": Reconciliation

Are there some crimes that cannot be forgiven? Are there evils that should not be reconciled? Are there enemies that fall outside the embrace of divine mercy? These deeper questions haunted Simon Wiesenthal, a young Jew in Nazi Germany. Detained in a prison camp, he was placed on janitorial detail and sent to work in a temporary hospital for wounded German soldiers. There he encountered a young soldier, mortally wounded and wrapped in bandages. The dying soldier could neither see nor speak, but he desperately sought forgiveness. The soldier confessed a terrible crime to Wiesenthal.

With his comrades, he had set fire to a building filled with Jewish families. As one family tried to escape the inferno, he shot them, and their deaths haunted him still. The faces gathered before his eyes as he lay dying. The soldier knew he needed to confess his crime to a Jew, and he begged Wiesenthal to forgive him. Wiesenthal left the room without a word.

Years later, Wiesenthal's refusal to forgive came back to haunt him. Should he have forgiven the dying soldier? Was forgiveness his to grant, or did that gift belong only to the direct victims of the soldier's crime? If he could not grant forgiveness, should he have spoken to the dying man? Could he have touched him? Does this encounter between a dying Nazi soldier and a Jewish prisoner delineate the limits of forgiveness?[3] These question so haunted Wiesenthal that he told the story and invited Jewish and Christian theologians and philosophers to respond, assembling their responses into a volume titled *The Sunflower*. The essays explore various dimensions of forgiveness, but the one I want to focus on here is forgiving the enemy.

The hardest sayings in the Gospels challenge disciples to extend forgiveness to the enemy and turn it into love. "Love your enemies; pray for those who persecute you." As these words were written, Christians suffered the first waves of persecution that hit their early communities. The command to "love your enemies" fell hard on disciples facing martyrdom:

> You have heard that it was said, "An eye for an eye and a tooth for a tooth." But I say to you, Do not resist an evildoer. But if anyone strikes you on the right cheek, turn the other also; and if anyone wants to sue you and take your coat, give your cloak as well; and if anyone forces you to go one mile, go also the second mile. Give to everyone who begs from you, and do not refuse any-one who wants to borrow from you.
>
> You have heard that it was said, "You shall love your neighbor and hate your enemy." But I say to you, Love your enemies and pray for those who persecute you, so that you may be children of your Father in heaven; for he makes his sun rise on the evil and on the good, and sends rain on the righteous and on the unrighteous. For if you love those who love you, what reward do you have? Do not even the tax collectors do the same? And if you greet only your brothers and sisters, what more are you doing than others? Do not even the Gentiles do the same? Be perfect, therefore, as your heavenly Father is perfect [Matthew 5:38–48].

Commanding love of the enemy in a time of persecution turned the canons of justice upside down.

The words counsel "tough love," as fit the times. The ancient world followed an etiquette of abuse, if one can imagine such a thing. Slaves and servants were usually struck with the back of the hand; peers and equals with the front of the hand. In a largely right-handed population, masters hit their subordinates on the right cheek with the back of the hand. In challenging people to "turn the other cheek," Jesus suggested a gesture of defiance. The only way to receive a blow on the right cheek would be from the palm of the master's hand. Turning the other cheek forced a master to acknowledge a slave as an equal.

There is more tough love in the command ordering Christians to "go the extra mile." By law, Roman soldiers could force people in the countries they occupied to carry their burdens one mile—but no more. Challenging his audience to continue for the second mile, Jesus again presented a gesture of defiance. The offer forced Romans to violate their own laws. Practicing tough love, disciples turn unjust laws and customs upside down. Jesus' commandments seem to grant advantage to the enemy; in fact, they bestow agency on the underdogs, giving them a way to fight back without violence.

Tough love topples the ancient law of the desert, which urged limit and moderation: "Just *one* eye for an eye, just *one* tooth for a tooth." Love reigns in its place. Love is the disciples' gesture of defiance in a world that threatens to implode in hatred. Forgiveness arrests a cycle of violence and points all parties toward reconciliation.

Note that the enemy may still be regarded as the enemy. Jesus did not recommend pretending that the enemy be magically morphed into friend or family. My colleague Ann, victim of a vicious betrayal, puts the distinction well: "I have forgiven them. That doesn't mean I have to trust them with my life. Believe me, I don't. I don't know if I could be friends with any of those people again. I am working to love them as my enemies." While respecting the distance that violation creates, Jesus nonetheless pushed for the quality of relationship to alter: "Love your enemies, pray for those who persecute you."

This gesture of defiance fits with everything Jesus did in the Gospels. Throughout his earthly ministry, Jesus related without discrimination to people in need. It mattered little to him whether some among his followers regarded others as enemies. He healed the servant of a Roman centurion, and the Romans were enemies to the Jews. He resuscitated the daughter of a leader of the synagogue, and the religious leaders were enemies to many of Jesus' disciples. He spoke with women, not just his own countrywomen but Samaritan and Syro-Phoenician women, people who were enemies to the Jews. He dined with tax collectors and sinners one night, Pharisees another. He chided a rich young man and then repaired to the home of wealthy friends, Mary, Martha, and Lazarus, to scrape off the road dust. Rich and poor, Jew and Gentile, women and men, righteous and sinner—each of these groups was at odds with the other. Jesus showed kindness to all. Perhaps the message he intended to get across to his disciples was simply this: "If you travel with me, you cannot afford to have enemies: it will be too confusing to keep track of who they are."

There is another complication in cataloguing enemies, and it echoes a lawyer's eagerness to create a taxonomy of neighbors. When he asked Jesus, "Who is my neighbor?" the question was turned back on him: "Are you a good neighbor?" Like the term *neighbor, enemy* is another term that defies easy categorization. As we rush to catalogue our enemies, we may behave as enemies in the eyes of others.

As the New Testament defines them, enemies are not only people whom we hate but also people who hate us. Remembering Matthew's Gospel, we realize that we must not consider only people whom we have "something against" but also people who have something against us. Who considers us an enemy? When Jesus asked his disciples to remember the people who have something against them, he reminded them that they might be enemies to someone else. This must have been shocking but nonetheless true.

A man in a course I taught on Christian practices discovered this insight quite by accident. I asked students to adopt a practice for the duration of the course and to commit themselves to doing it on a daily basis. I participated along with them. Every week, we would report on our practices, a kind of group spiritual direction. This man chose as his practice prayer for his enemies. He readily confessed to using the practice for ulterior motives: new insights, eased relationships, and some measure of compassion. To some degree, these benefits materialized. As the semester advanced, however, the man discovered that the practice itself held some surprises. Most unsettling was the way he began to see himself as an enemy in his easy ability to generate ill will toward people he disliked. He found that he needed to reconcile his judgmental tendencies with the call to "love your enemies; pray for those who persecute you." In short, the man needed to admit his weakness, ask for forgiveness, and make amends. As he learned to love others, he learned to love that part of himself that "othered" people, that turned them into outsiders, strangers, and outcasts. He discovered the enemy within.

In the aftermath of September 11, 2001, citizens of the United States made a similar discovery. Initially, the numbers of dead and the magnitude of the destruction took people's breath away. "How could anyone do this to us?" In time, the answer became painfully clear. As people began to assimilate reactions from around the world, Americans realized that their country was perceived as an enemy by many of the world's people. Criticized for its foreign policy and foreign aid decisions, its unilateralism, its trade relations, and its standard of living light-years beyond that of the world's poorest countries, the United States came to realize that it was not universally well regarded. Many voices could not resist recrimination: "We live with this every day! Now you see what it's like." "You never cared about Afghanistan before—now that you perceive it as a threat, you want to liberate the Afghani people? You'll leave when you capture your prey." Americans were at odds with too many of the world's people. How can political decisions position people to work toward reconciliation, particularly when every impulse tends toward recrimination?

In a world that is not yet according to God, virtue is not always rewarded, and enemies abound on all sides. Forgiveness ranks as one of the most difficult practices of discipleship. Even when disciples can muster forgiveness, it does not always effect reconciliation. Maybe sometimes it shouldn't. Evil is its own mystery, and it possesses the power to enthrall. When forgiveness fails, we call on the light of Christ to disperse the darkness.

Several years ago I reviewed a book on the theological dimensions of evil. It was a terrific book; in fact, it was a little too good. I caught myself reading with more than academic interest accounts of everything from petty vice to more serious sin to Satanic rituals. As I devoured the book's contents, I realized that I myself was being devoured. Quite literally, I was enthralled by the subject matter. It felt like being sucked down a drain, like trying to breathe while being suffocated.

The insights of Saint Augustine suddenly made sense. Evil, he wrote, is the absence of good. Like a vacuum, it sucks the breath out of every living thing. In the face of such horror, there are only two alternatives: to join it or to defy it. Love defies evil, breathing life into people deadened by recrimination. Loving the enemy places a roadblock in the path of revenge.

Is love always possible? Are disciples being asked to do something beyond their capabilities? The answer to these questions lies in the crucifixion. Too often Jesus' words from the cross play with "Hallelujah" choruses in the background: we fast-forward to Easter. In fact, the forces of evil gathered at the foot of the cross. Jesus felt himself abandoned by friends, followers, even his beloved Father. He stared into the abyss of evil. His choice was clear: join it or defy it. He defied evil with a gesture of forgiveness: "Father, forgive them, for they know not what they do" (Luke 23:34).

We like to think that Jesus spoke with compassion, but he may well have spit these words out. I hope he was human enough to feel all the recrimination to which he was entitled, and I'll bet he struggled with the unnatural character of forgiveness just like any human being. Whether his tone was one of mercy or recrimination, the words themselves shock us. The man who taught his disciples to love their enemies could not measure up himself. Jesus did not say, "I forgive you; I love you," and he did not utter the words because he could not. The Romans, the temple guards, the disciples: everyone betrayed him, and the wrong done to him unjustly, undeservedly, overwhelmed him. He could not forgive all of this evil on his own. From the dark space of abandonment, Jesus called out for a love greater than his own: "Father, forgive them." With these words, he asked God to forgive what he could not. He called on divine love when his own capacity to love failed him.

If Jesus could not forgive, what hope is there for us? When Jesus had reached the limits of his own compassion, he appealed to the source of all compassion. He found the capacity to forgive, not from within himself, but from the One who sent him. The forgiveness of Jesus from the cross stands as a stunning example to all disciples. When all else fails and our frail powers of repenting, remembering, and loving have been completely paralyzed, we ask God to forgive our enemies until we can forgive them on our own.

In a letter to his friend Malcolm, C. S. Lewis recalls the cruelty of a schoolmaster who had for years inflicted physical and emotional abuse on him and his schoolmates. The schoolmaster had long since died, but the memory of his abuse stayed with Lewis. Lewis turned the matter over to prayer. He writes, "Last week while at prayer, I suddenly discovered—or felt as if I did—that I had really forgiven someone I had been trying to forgive for over thirty years. Trying and praying that I might."[4] Lewis called on the forgiveness of God to help him when his own powers fell short. Over time he found forgiveness; over time forgiveness found him.

Thirty years may seem like a long time to be on the road to forgiveness, and Lewis was still not certain of closure. Some people never find forgiveness, and they bear into adulthood childhood wounds that have never healed. What prompted Lewis to turn the practice of forgiveness over to God? Perhaps he found himself unable to forgive, and he prayed for the ability to forgive. Perhaps he found himself unwilling to forgive, and he prayed for the desire to forgive. Whatever he prayed for, he kept praying. Eventually, forgiveness found him.

The closure that we seek comes with the heavenly banquet, when we sit at table with friend and foe alike, to dine in the presence of the Trinity. The heavenly meal clarifies why we need earthly forgiveness. We have to speak with our seatmates, who may have been our enemies in an earthly life. In their truest selves, those seated at our right and left hands are children of God, and we need to treat them as such. The practice of forgiveness prepares us for the etiquette of the heavenly banquet, where we will dine with one another as forgiven forgivers.

· · · · · · · · · · · · · · · · · · · · · · · · · · · · · · · ·

# Remembering

## *Loving with a Resurrection Affection*

The day after Halloween, my pumpkin had half its face eaten away. I thought this might have been the prank of some trick-or-treater with a strange appetite and an even stranger sense of humor. I began to think uncharitably of the neighborhood children. By the next day, the whole face had disappeared. I started suspecting some supernatural appetite. All the other pumpkins on all the neighbors' porches were intact, saggy but still smiling their toothy grins. My pumpkin alone was being devoured.

My mind raced into anxiety overdrive. My husband was away on business, and I was alone in the house. His good spirits, I am always convinced, work better than a truckload of garlic in warding off vampires and evil vapors. Maybe in his absence, demons had returned seven times stronger than before.

Surely my house was possessed. I ransacked memory and inspection reports for information on other owners. I remembered that a prior owner dug out the basement to build himself a stained-glass studio. How could we have been gullible enough to believe this? The studio now seemed more sinister than artsy. I wondered if there was something under the floor of the basement laundry room. Had some unquiet soul returned to register revenge—and failed to check the mailbox for a change of address? Was my house haunted?

After a fitful sleep, I awoke to find the pumpkin utterly gone. Now my anxiety was complete. The horror escalated. Demons targeted not simply my house but my person. I now knew what was rustling in the magnolia tree in a night of no wind. I now knew why a car had churned up the street in the middle of the night— only to turn and careen back down. Evils spirits had devoured my pumpkin—and I was next. I was haunted.

Closer inspection revealed no supernatural being but the familiar red squirrel who has claimed the front yard as his turf. He had rolled the pumpkin off the porch railing and into the garden. When I found it later, I identified tiny teeth marks, a telltale sign of his munching. This territorial rodent ate everything in sight. Summer's end made him especially ravenous, and he scurried to add winter weight. The sinister scenario I had conjured evaporated—and the squirrel wars began.

I was haunted nevertheless—not by squirrels or spirits but haunted, as all disciples are, by that larger communion of saints whom we will one day join. This chapter resurrects an ancient practice: remembering the dead. In the earliest centuries of Christianity, persecution and martyrdom created saints of men and women who had died proclaiming the dangerous message that Jesus Christ was Lord. Their memory sustained those who were left behind. It so strengthened the fragile communities of earliest Christians that one theologian exclaimed, "The blood of the martyrs is the seed of the church!" Persecution made the church stronger and deepened the conviction of ordinary disciples.

By the early Middle Ages, the cult of the saints took on a life of its own, featuring a pantheon of superheroes whose cult at times rivaled devotion to the Crucified One. Protestant Christians largely dismissed the cult for a devotion they feared idolatrous. But in so doing, I fear that Protestant Christians lost an awareness of the sustaining guidance that the communion of saints offers to disciples in the present. The saints are not idols but tutors. In a world according to God, they guide us in discipleship of the One who calls out to us: "Follow me."

This chapter revisits the cult of the saints. I include as saints not simply the men and women beatified and canonized by pontifical process but also those ordinary saints whose love for us crosses the grave's divide. These departed disciples sustain us on the journey that they have faithfully completed. Since they are so much with us and for us, those who "have died in the Lord" are not really dead. They live to teach us, and their living witness makes these ordinary saints vehicles of resurrection hope.

When sainthood coalesces with discipleship, we become haunted in a good way, because the saints always attend us. Remembering them remains an important practice in Christian discipleship. If we had ears to hear, we could hear them speaking Jesus' parting words of assurance to his disciples: "And remember, we are with you always, to the close of the age" (Matthew 28:20). In probing the Christian practice of remembering the dead, we living disciples cherish those who have died. At first glance, the invitation seems unfamiliar, even scary, but we decline it to our peril. The saints have much to teach us, if only we will stop to listen. The dead teach us to live; they teach us to love aright; most surprisingly, they teach us to dance.

## Teaching Us How to Live

The dead teach us to live, and they do so in gracious ways. Their first lesson shows us how porous the border is between their world and our own. Through dreams, prayers, and memory, the dead walk among the living. They invite us to view the world according to God, literally from a God's-eye view. From this altered horizon, the dead also instruct the living in the ways of peace, a second lesson. When he returned to his disciples from the realm of the dead, the resurrected Jesus greeted them with the words "Peace be with you." Resurrection peace is God's final word against violence.

### A Lesson About Borders

To harvest the first lesson the dead have to teach, we need to recall the faithfulness of female saints who attended Jesus in his last hours. These women are long dead, but their devotion remains. Jesus traveled with a large entourage of women, but the Gospel accounts leave them largely nameless. In the crucifixion and resurrection stories, however, they step out of the shadows to claim agency: Mary Magdalene, Mary the mother of James, Mary the mother of Jesus, Joanna, Salome, "the other Mary." The women who surrounded Jesus in life did not abandon him in death. They went to the tomb early in the morning, and they arrived to find the tomb empty and the body gone. An angel announced the resurrection almost as a rebuke: "Why seek ye the living among the dead?" (Luke 24:5, King James Version).

The angel's question dumbfounded these faithful women. They sought Jesus, but if the angel was right, they were looking in the wrong places. Suddenly the ordered boundaries between the realms of the living and the dead fell away. The one whom they laid in a tomb three days ago now lived. They would not find him here.

"Why seek ye the living among the dead?" The question catapults across the centuries to confound disciples even today. We too seek life, but we are often confused about where to look. Part of the confusion lies in a chronic inability to distinguish between life and death. No clear border separates the lands of the living and the dead, and no ordinary map charts these territories. Sometimes the dead appear among the living—and sometimes the living appear to be dead.

Pope John Paul II, head of the Roman Catholic Church, challenges the "culture of death" that pervades much of modern culture. He offers as evidence everything from abortion to genocide, from grinding poverty to capital punishment. Disciples of different stripes might well disagree with the pope's position on the particulars, but no one escapes the insight. The world indeed traffics in a "culture of death."

The distribution of wealth between rich and poor contributes to a culture of death. I recall a conversation with a young Nigerian Christian about the "right to life." We talked for several minutes before realizing we both referred to very different kinds of life. In my context, "right to life" described a position opposed to the practice of abortion. The "life" referred to here meant fetal life. My conversation partner spoke from a context where "right to life" described the fragile hold newborn children had on life. Famine, disease, and infant mortality diminished their chances of surviving childhood. In a country where women fought to keep their children alive, the practice of abortion was incomprehensible. Where is the border between the living and the dead in these two cultural contexts?

Here is another example, from a lawyer with whom I swim. She counts herself among the "walking dead." She wonders aloud if her enviable salary compensates work that she describes without hesitation as "deadening" and "soul-destroying." Barraged by petty cases from litigious clients, she navigates a sea of suspicion concerning people's motives. "Most days I see the worst of human nature," she sighs. She struggles to persuade herself that her clients' world is not the only one that exists. "I need to get out of this job before I lose my ability to hope," she says. Where is the border between the realm of the dead and the realm of the living in this woman's life? The young lawyer felt she found the dead among the living—and feared that she would join them.

At other times the living appear among the dead. I resurrect from memory Grandmother Stortz, my father's mother, who lived with the family when I was six years old. My father was the child of her middle age. By the time I appeared on the scene, his mother must have been well into her seventies. She was already gray-haired and creaky with arthritis. I never saw Grandmother Stortz wearing anything other than a freshly ironed print housedress, black stack heels, and stockings. Though life had given her little to laugh about, she always looked as if she were remembering a good joke.

Age and dress confer a certain formality, but Grandmother Stortz discarded it every Saturday morning. Planted in front of a small black-and-white television, she tuned in to wrestling—"wrassling," she called it. My father returned from his yard work to find his mother in her print housedress and black pumps colorfully cheering on a pair of hulking athletes with names as false as their talents. His two young daughters sat at her feet mesmerized, cheering their granny on.

Somewhere in her eighties Grandmother Stortz lost interest in wrassling. It was probably around this time that her granddaughters lost interest in watching television with her. Other activities occupied their Saturday mornings. Grandma Stortz took to the newspapers, restricting her reading to the obituary columns. Every morning at breakfast, she would wonder aloud, "Well, let's see who died in the papers." I grew up thinking the *Baltimore Sun* could be a lethal weapon, at least to the unhappy souls who'd somehow met their fate in its pages.

Where most people tried to restrict death to funeral homes, Grandma Stortz invited it to breakfast. Of course, eventually she "died in the papers" too. Her own long, richly textured life was distilled into the tiny print and florid prose of an obituary. I remember her every time I read the obits—and I find myself laughing. I suppose it is all her fault that I find the living, quite literally, among the dead. In ways both great and small, we do find the dead among the living and the living among the dead. And if the border between living and dead fades in and out of focus, how do we "seek the living"? Where should we begin to look?

We can begin by looking for ways of living that promote life. Again and again, the saints remind us: "See, I am setting before you the way of life and the way of death" (Jeremiah 21:8). The prophet Jeremiah seemed well acquainted with the "walking dead," as the young lawyer put it. He charged the faithful to "execute justice in the morning, and deliver from the hand of the oppressor anyone who has been robbed, or else my wrath will go forth like fire, and burn, with no one to quench it, because of your evil doings" (Jeremiah 21:12). Anyone who expected high heavenly drama to descend on those who chose the way of death would be sorely disappointed. Their fate was quieter and more perilous. Those who chose the way of death were punished by their own actions. Injustice destroyed their souls; they lived as if they were dead.

Moral instruction in the ancient world featured language about "two ways," and they were variously described as "a way of life" and "a way of death" or "a way of light" and "a way of darkness." In the Synoptic Gospels, Jesus tapped into this rich moral conversation with brief parables about wise men who built their houses on rock and foolish men who built on sand (Matthew 7:24–27), about healthy or unhealthy eyes that filled the body with light or darkness (Matthew 6:22–23), about easy paths that led to destruction and hard paths that led to life (Matthew 7:13–14; Luke 13:23–24).

People today still use this language of "two ways" when they speak of someone "turning her life around" or of someone "taking a turn for the worse." People trip merrily "down the primrose path" or "head in the wrong direction." Still others have the misfortune to look "like forty miles of bad road." Exactly what lies at the end of the road is unclear, but these phrases hint at paths that lead to destruction or health.

The New Testament tells disciples both the destination and the road that leads to it. John's Gospel proclaims Jesus himself as "the way, the truth, and the life" (John 14:6). Jesus is both the road and its destination. On the one hand, Jesus' statement was completely outrageous. It dismantled all prior maps that claimed to chart the two ways. On the other, his statement offered disciples then and now what Robert Frost called "a momentary stay against confusion."[1] In a world where the border between the living and the dead seems porous, where the dead move among the living and the living move as people long dead, it is a comfort to know where to find life, abundant life: Jesus.

### A Lesson About Peace

The dead also teach us about peace, God's final word against violence. A common epitaph on gravestones reads "Rest in peace." Most of the headstones in a cemetery bear these weighty words, and they are usually understood as the family's fervent wish for the departed. If one could eavesdrop on conversations among the mourners who come to remember the dead, many of them would be about how some poor departed soul "is finally at peace." The remark could refer to a wasting disease that made someone's final months miserable to a string of unresolved estrangements that brought an embittered family to the funeral. It could also invoke the simple wisdom that living well is both a grace and an uphill battle. "Rest in peace" stands as a final benediction spoken by the living to the dead.

But let's imagine for a moment that the words do not address the dead. Rather the words speak to us, the living, and they challenge us to spend our time making peace. Instead of being the mourners' blessing for their dearly departed, the words "Rest in peace" stand as the final counsel from the dead to the living. Imagine what these bones would say if they could speak. "We have seen it all, and we know that peace is the only way to live. Resist violence; reconcile with your enemies; love without measure." These are the last words of the dead to the living—and we need them.

An old rancher in Missoula took this advice while he was still alive. Relocated to the city so that he could be close to his chemotherapy, he had to abandon his farm, his cattle, and the landscapes he had grown to love. He knew his days were numbered, and he called the extended family to his bedside. There was still time, he announced, to put aside grudges great and small. He bade all disgruntled parties to be reconciled to one another. "I'll say it: my family got to know me a lot better. It made better people out of us. I went to my brother and my sister and my in-laws and said, You know there's no hope for ever healing me up or getting me well. Now, do you want to get along and not fight over whose rooster that is over there? It has changed us for the better. We've straightened things out for the better—for sure not for the worse."[2] The rancher tried to leave his family and his family affairs in peace, asking them to rest in a greater peace than they had experienced up to that point. As they remember him, they will remember also his example of reconciliation. His final counsel to them was to "Rest in peace."

The words echo Jesus' first words to his disciples after the resurrection: "Peace be with you" (John 20:19). These were the same disciples who had deserted him in death, fleeing the scene of the crucifixion. Nor did the faithless disciples attend Jesus' burial, leaving preparation of the body to the women, Joseph of Arimathea, and the despised tax collector Nicodemus. After the resurrection, the disciples huddled in a room behind locked doors, lest Jewish or Roman authorities find them and subject them to Jesus' fate. The person they most longed for was also the person they most feared. And suddenly he was in their midst. Before anyone could utter a word, Jesus said it all: "Peace be with you." He had to say it twice before the disciples were able to calm down. Jesus came to them with the wisdom of the dead: "Rest in peace."

These words fall hard on a warlike world. Nation struggles against nation in the Middle East, in Central Asia, in the Korean peninsula. A body of "united nations" confronts a threat that disregards the boundaries of sovereign nations: transnational terrorism. Finding the way out of a labyrinth of death seems impossible. Perhaps Jesus' way of dealing with the disciples offers a partial solution across the world's religions. First, find peace within your troubled souls, lest you project your inner divisions outward. For Christians, peace means clinging to the One who promised to be "the way, the truth, and the life." If disciples find that peace within their hearts, they will project peace outwardly.

## Teaching Us How to Love

Remembering the dead reorders our affections. The dead teach us to love aright; they teach us a resurrection affection. In many ways, this is a costly lesson. After the crucifixion, Mary Magdalene arrived at Jesus' tomb to find it empty, and she was profoundly troubled. Her pain intensified when Jesus appeared and told her she could no longer touch him: "Do not hold on to me" (John 20:17). His words told her that their relationship had altered in ways she literally could no longer grasp. Jesus was no less present to her, but she had to relinquish the comfort of physical touch. She had to learn to love Jesus all over again.

The rest of the disciples faced the same problem. Learning a resurrection affection presented a steep learning curve, but Jesus proved to be a gentle teacher. His final appearance to the disciples in the Gospel of John eerily echoes the first encounter beside the Sea of Galilee. The disciples had returned to their nets. This time they have been fishing all night, catching nothing. A man appeared on the shore and told them where to cast their nets. They did not recognize Jesus immediately. But when the catch exceeded the capacity of their nets, the disciples understood they were in the presence of the risen Christ. They associated Jesus with abundance. When they reached the shore, Jesus was calmly cooking them breakfast.

After a meal, Jesus gave the disciples a lesson in resurrection affection. The lesson started badly. Once again Peter was clueless, but Jesus kept pressing the question, "Do you love me?" The questioning gave Peter a chance to take back each of his three denials on that awful night when Jesus was taken prisoner. But Jesus also gave Peter—and the rest of us disciples—some hints about resurrection affection. Jesus told Peter to love him by tending his sheep, by feeding his sheep—in short, by following him. He would not be around in the accustomed ways. Loving Jesus long distance and without the comfort of physical presence meant loving the people he left behind.

Loving long distance challenges anyone who has been bereaved. Sometimes the pain is so great that people work to forget. Others blunt their memories by busyness or denial or anger or a quick replacement. For those who brave the country of memory, the pain is always fresh. A friend whom I had not seen for quite a while remembered her father's death with such vivid detail, I asked if he had died recently. "No," she answered, surprising herself. "He died almost ten years ago, although it feels like just yesterday." A world of sadness lay close to the surface. As she talked more, though, she spoke of a different kind of presence. "He was ill for a long, long time, and he kind of receded from our lives. For years afterward I could only dream about him as I last knew him: sick and diminished. My dreams were filled with anxiety: Could I get him to a hospital? Did he have enough to eat? Was he comfortable? It took many years before I could dream him whole again, and now he almost always appears in my dreams as the vigorous man he was in my youth." She also recounted an experience common to the newly bereaved. Shortly after her father died, she had a sense of her father's presence, stronger than mere yearning, less definite than an apparition. Reluctant to categorize it, she said only, "I knew he was there, and I knew he was all right." That sense of her father's presence overwhelmed the terrible feeling of loss. "For so long he was so diminished. I felt like I suddenly had him back in essence—and there was such love."

My friend expressed a common experience eloquently. It brought to my mind an interview on television with a mother whose daughter had died in the attack on the World Trade Center towers. After the towers were hit, she had left a message on her mother's answering machine. The mother spent the first hours after the incident trying to determine her daughter's fate. In the middle of the night, a bolt of light shot through the apartment. "In a big city like New York, you're never in darkness, but this was different," the mother recounted. "There was nothing that could have made this light—I'd never seen it before. I knew at once that my daughter had died, and I knew that she was all right." She shook her head, as if she still could not digest these conflicting pieces of information, then repeated the words more slowly: "I just knew she was all right."

A resurrection affection reaches across death's divide. From the "other side," the dead love us and attract our affection in return.

The challenge for those of us who are left behind is to respond in ways that cannot depend on physical contact or verbal expression but in their silence are no less real.

The need for a resurrection affection marked the earliest Christians, only they had no answering machines to prompt their memory. As martyrdom systematically thinned their ranks, these early disciples faced severe loss. Often they were rejected by their families of origin, cut off and cut out. Then disciples watched as the family of brothers and sisters in Christ, their alternative family, was decimated by persecution. The early Christian martyrs suffered unspeakable horrors, and they found strength to persevere in the resurrected Christ. They did not simply follow Christ's example; they felt Christ was in them, suffering on their behalf. Christ shouldered their tortures, and to a person, they testified, "It is not I but Christ who will be suffering in me." Like the women who went to Jesus' tomb to tell stories and mourn, the Christians who survived persecution gathered at the tombs of the martyrs. Gradually these sites evolved into places of healing, exorcism, and devotion. Friendship with the saints and martyrs transformed an earthly camaraderie. Christians developed ways of loving long distance, and they dubbed the martyrs "the friends of God." No longer physically accessible, these invisible friends accompanied their earthly counterparts through prayer and patronage.

Cults developed around local saints, people whom a first generation of martyrdom had known personally. Christians would gather at the tombs of these comrades, remembering them, telling stories, asking for their aid. Love of these local heroes bound together the communities they had left behind, and people searched to find ways to express their enduring affection.

It is also not surprising that the love of friendship came to characterize this resurrection affection. Friendship demands a kind of distance for its flourishing. While erotic love erases boundaries in an ecstasy of physical abandon, friendship cherishes boundaries. In respecting the differences between people, friendship safeguards

the individuality of the other. For this reason the Greek philosophers regarded friendship as the most refined form of loving.
Following their lead, twentieth-century philosopher and mystic
Simone Weil writes of friendship as a "miracle," the miracle by
which "a person consents to view from a certain distance, and without coming any nearer, the very being who is necessary to him as
food."[3] When we think about the distance death imposes between
people who love one another, Weil's observation makes a lot of
sense. Those who have died—mothers and fathers, husbands and
wives, partners and friends—are surely as necessary to us as eating.
Death imposes an unwelcome distance that love struggles to bridge.
These earliest Christians reached across the chasm of death to
befriend their saints. As they remembered them, they gained practice in a resurrection affection.

Gradually, a cult of the saints supplanted these early cults of the
martyrs, featuring prayers and remembering. Reformation churches
reacted variously to a cult that had been a vital part of medieval
spirituality. In England, where people debated whether pope or
monarch should head the church, Catholic saints simply became
Anglican ones. On the Continent, however, the cult of the saints
faced greater dangers. Martin Luther abhorred the commercialism
that had grown to surround these cults, but he acknowledged the
deep human need for these "invisible friends." In his commentaries
on scripture, particularly his work on Genesis, he clearly represented
the Old Testament figures like Joseph, Abraham, and Dinah as
everyday saints. More radical reformers dispensed with saints
altogether, tearing down statues from churches, melting down their
reliquaries, collecting their bones and burning them. Horrified by
this sacrilege, the Roman Catholic king of Spain, Philip II, sent
emissaries into Protestant Europe to salvage saints' relics. He displayed the retrieved relics in his great palace outside the city of
Madrid, El Escorial, alongside the bodies of the former kings and
queens of Spain. Built to represent architecturally the grid on which
Saint Lawrence was martyred, El Escorial was a palace of death

where Masses for the dead were said almost continuously, a perpetual memorial.

Devotion to the saints continues to this day—perhaps because the saints are so devoted to us. Author Ron Hansen writes of his love of the long dead British poet Gerard Manley Hopkins, whom he regarded as an intercessor. Hansen was offered an endowed chair at a prestigious university. The only hitch was that he already had a job that he liked and that afforded him time to write. As he debated internally the pros and cons of the two positions, he invoked the counsel of his intercessor through prayer. The next evening, the president of the university phoned for a decision. Hansen recalled the conversation: "'We'll call it the Gerard Manley Hopkins chair. Does that mean anything to you?' It did. And I imagined Gerard in heaven, smiling."[4]

Like so many Christians in centuries past, Hansen found that he had been assisted by an "invisible friend," someone whose elegance of thought and expression compelled him. I suspect that if they had words to say it, many Christians could report similar experiences with such "invisible friends." Their saints may not have received official canonization or even written great poetry, but Christians depend on the affection of people beyond the grave, whether by direct intercession or quiet recollection. In love that stretches across the grave's divide, the dead teach us how to love.

## Teaching Us How to Dance

The earliest Christians used to gather at the graves of their local martyrs to eat and drink and tell stories. These graveside festivals were a popular North African sport. Persecution had been fierce in the region, and remembering the dead was a gesture of resistance. By celebrating their martyrs, Christians thumbed their noses at the governing authorities.

The practice took hold. Even after persecution ended, Christians gathered on feast days at the graves of the martyrs to eat, drink, be merry, and remember. The great North African theologian, Augustine of Hippo, remembers how fond his mother was of this practice. She took it with her to Italy, where she followed the career of her brilliant son. Mother Monica was admonished by none other than the great Christian bishop Ambrose of Milan that "this was not the Italian way." But even Ambrose, with all his honeyed words, could not tamp down the resilience of a custom Christians found life-giving: remembering the dead. Then as now, Christians are a haunted people: we refuse to be parted from our dead.

The dead also refuse to be parted from the living. Similar hauntings captured the imagination of late medieval Christians. Throughout northern Europe, cathedral and cloister walls depicted an odd celebration. Called the *Totentanz* or *danse macabre*, the paintings displayed what was a disturbing dance. Gathered in a circle among tombstones were the dead and the living, hand in hand, dancing on the graves. The dead dance with a fluid grace. Madly grinning, they are nothing but bones. It is impossible to tell who these folks are. No clothes allow for identification of gender or class, status or family. Indeed, watching the dance brings to mind words of the apostle Paul. The passage is familiar—but never invoked in this context: "There is no longer Jew or Greek, there is no longer slave or free, there is no longer male and female; for all of you are one in Christ" (Galatians 3:28). The democracy of death makes no distinctions.

The living people in these pictures are easier to sort out. We see men and women, rich and poor, nobles and serfs. By their dress shall you know them! Clothes and possessions identify the status of the living all too clearly. For all their distinctiveness, the living are infinitely more disturbing. They are the ones who are unable to move freely. They are more encumbered than the dead, and they stumble through the dance. They trip over clothes; their money chests and tools get in the way; their friends try to pull them out of the dance. They are not quite certain they want to dance with one another. A nobleman withholds his hand from a peasant; a serf looks with alarm at her partner, a knight. If the living appear worried by their this-worldly partners, they are visibly anxious about dancing with the dead. They all appear appalled by the situation in which they find themselves. Shock does not lend itself to grace.

The dance of death presents a riveting performance, outrageous and fascinating at the same time. As one looks longer, though, there is something wildly comforting and deeply true about the whole scene. The dead live more fully and more freely than the living. They cavort and bound as if filled with a joy that does not belong to this world. The onlooker feels a little wistful: it is clear who in these paintings is having all the fun. And one realizes that our possessions and our wealth, our fine titles and full résumés finally fail to satisfy. The dead teach us to travel light and listen hard—listen for strains of the hymns sung constantly at the throne of the Lamb: "Blessings and glory and wisdom and thanksgiving and honor and power and might, be to our God forever and ever!" (Revelation 7:12). Now *there* is a song to dance to! If we look at these mixed couples, living and dead, this is what we learn.

We learn something else as well. The dead lead the living in the dance; they are the dance instructors. They have taken the living gently but firmly in their grasp. The dead lead the living in a dance that we will all make someday, sooner or later, with more and less grace—and we had better start practicing our moves now.

The cynic could dismiss all of these hauntings as products of an imagination made morbid by the plague and famine that swept through Europe in this time. But one could also regard these paintings as statements of faith. Our modern-day hospice movements are born of the conviction that no one should die alone. These medieval artists tell us quite matter-of-factly that no one does. At every moment, we have these supernatural partners beside us—if only we will confess that we are haunted. Call it haunted by grace, if you will, but grace comes as it often does: in the faces of the people we love.

Several years ago I caught a radio interview on *West Coast Weekend* with author Tobias Wolff. He was talking to an interviewer who clearly found his Catholicism "quaint." "Would you consider yourself a Catholic writer?" she asked. "Does being a Catholic affect your writing?" The way she put the questions, it was quite clear that the answers she expected were "No!" and "Not much." Wolff paused—you could almost hear the interviewer squirming. Finally, he responded quietly: "When you're a Catholic, the world is a much more crowded place." He spoke with all the authority of one who is regularly haunted by those in this other communion, the communion of saints. Wolff went on to speak of a conspiracy of memory and prayer that offers us contact with that other community in which we too will someday reside.

## A Haunted People

As Christians, we live as a haunted people. For us the world is a very crowded place. In conclusion, I want to take two steps. Since we are all beginners in this dance, I will make them very simple. The first step moves back to the dance of death that so transfixed the medieval imagination. The site of this dancing—the dance floor, if you will—is the body of Christ. We listen again to words of the apostle Paul, writing this time to the Romans: "Do you not know that all of us who have been baptized into Christ Jesus were baptized into his death? Therefore we have been buried with him by baptism into death, so that, just as Christ was raised from the dead by the glory of the Father, so we too might walk in newness of life" (Romans 6:3–4). My teenage nieces would say, "The world according to God rocks!" On the journey of discipleship, there is definitely dancing, and we dance in newness of life. As we proceed, singing and praying, eating and drinking, we join in a great celebration. The line dances to the tomb of Jesus, only that tomb is empty. Death is swallowed up in victory, and we dance at the conquest. If you look carefully, you probably dance with someone you love; someone whose presence you ache for leads you in the dance.

The second step leads us back to the Beatitudes, the Christian Bill of Rights that inaugurates Matthew's Sermon on the Mount: "Blessed are those who mourn, for they shall be comforted" (Matthew 5:4). In one of his inaugural blessings, Jesus remembers those who grieve and promises that they shall be comforted. Disciples know where that comfort comes from. The comfort promised comes from the very ones we mourn as they reach out to take us by the hand.

# 8

# Fidelity

## Promising Ourselves Body, Mind, Soul, and Spirit

Christians talk a lot about sex. A topic that used to be avoided in polite company now appears regularly in pulpits, Sunday school classrooms, and adult Bible studies. The conversations are spirited, opinionated, and often just plain angry. People wonder aloud if all this talk about sex will be "church-dividing." I maintain that if we speak out of the lifestyle of discipleship, Christian talk about sex can be church-uniting. More important, Christian talk about sex might just have both wisdom and a sense of humor.

My fear is that when Christians talk about sex, they uncritically adopt concepts that do not express the depth of their convictions. We talk about sexual identity as if it were the center of gravity for who we are. We discuss sexual behavior as a list of "thou shalt nots," warning people off certain behaviors without saying what sex should be in positive terms. We speak of sexual practices as a kind of containment policy: what not to do with what to whom. Is this the way Christians should be talking about sex? I think not.

Christian talk about sex starts with an identity we all share. It begins not in the bedroom but at the baptismal font. In fact, before we say anything at all, we should break bread and drink wine in memory of God's Son. Celebrating the body we share invites God into the conversation. It reminds Christians that we have a first language of faith. Speaking it with fluency has the potential to foster faithful conversation.

Faithful conversation about sexuality injects a passionate debate with some much needed discernment. First, sexuality is not a "gift," as so many church documents tout. Sexuality is simply a part of being human, along with eating, drinking, and aging. Baptism brings the whole person into relationship with the body of Christ and a body of believers through a symphony of promises. Second, fidelity is the practice of discipleship that safeguards sexuality. Fidelity depends on promises, because through promise-making and promise-keeping, people guarantee today who they will be tomorrow. Finally, the practice of fidelity suggests a sexual ethic for all who claim the lifestyle of discipleship, married or partnered, single or celibate. A sexual ethic of discipleship embraces dimensions of prayer, power, and all parts of the human person. In the lifestyle of discipleship, sexuality contributes to positive goods: faithfulness, generativity, and service. These are the "thou shalts" that Christian sexuality supports.

Fidelity is a central practice in discipleship. It touches all areas of the lifestyle of discipleship, not just matters sexual. Disciples keep faith to jobs and families, to communities and groups, to causes and projects. The identity conferred in baptism, of being a Christian, orients all of these complex commitments. Keeping faith in Christ's body gives unique guidance to Christian sexuality. Indeed, the primary orientation of Christians is to the body of Christ. Through examining the practice of fidelity this chapter develops the unique implications of baptismal identity for Christian sexual ethics.

## Sexuality: Help from the Font

Most contemporary church social statements about sex assert that sexuality is a "gift." This seems to be the way postmodern Christians clear their throats, assuring skeptics that they are neither prudish nor captive to centuries in which sexuality was dismissed as an embarrassment or an abomination.

However, in elevating sexuality to the status of "gift," Christians risk romanticizing or sacralizing sex. As one the earliest and earthiest of the Protestant reformers, Martin Luther presented a vivid argument against requiring celibacy for priests: "The pope has as little power to command this as he has to forbid eating, drinking, the natural movement of the bowels, or growing fat."[1] He brooked no romanticized or sacramentalized treatment of sexuality. It merited no more reverence than eating, drinking, defecating, and the general tendency of the body to "head south" over time, as a friend in his fifties described his physique. "It all seems to have gathered around my waist," he sighed. Forbidding sex was as futile as forbidding the natural process of aging. The real question was this: How could Christians be faithful in the midst of eating and drinking, aging and desire?

Christians would do well to adopt a healthy realism about sexuality. Gift language romanticizes and idealizes sexuality, making it all the more difficult to address its dangers: manipulation, teasing, withholding affection, objectification or manipulation, molestation, adultery, incest, rape. How many young people have been duped by this rhetoric, only to find their first sexual experience disappointing? It was rough, impersonal—and no one prepared them for all the mess. How many long-married people wonder if the sex they have is good enough, sexy enough, or simply enough? A forty-something-year-old woman walked out of a twenty-something-year-old marriage because she wanted "to be passionately in love at least once in my life." Beguiled by a culture that worships sex, she clearly thought she was missing something to which she was entitled. I fear she will find that the life she yearns for exists only within the covers of slick magazines. Realistic accounts of sexuality like Luther's offer a corrective to these romanticized accounts as well as a platform for addressing sexual abuses.

Baptism steers us in the right direction. Baptism—not sexuality—funds our primary identity, which orients other facets of our being.

Christians get lots of messages about their primary identity from the media, from their country, from various interest groups and causes that all compete to stake their claim. "You're an American!" "You're a Republican!" "You're a card-carrying member of the AARP!" "You're a gay man!" "You're a feminist!" "You're black—and proud!" Add to these the roles we inhabit, each vying for dominance, and the diversity becomes overwhelming. Each day begins a new decathlon as I struggle to be a writer, a speaker, a teacher, a housekeeper, a wife, a citizen—and yes, a swimmer. All these worthy identities pull in a dozen different directions, and I yearn for a center of gravity that will order the chaos. Several years ago a young scholar whom I had been invited to introduce gave me a valuable clue. She was quite adamant about her primary identity. She wanted to be introduced as a "feminist Christian" not a "Christian feminist." I asked about the difference, and she said with some conviction, "I want people to know where my center of gravity is. For me, 'Christian' is the dominant noun, not the modifying adjective." Christians receive their primary identity in baptism. This sense of who we are organizes all other facets of our personality, our lives, our interactions with others. By incorporating Christians into the body of Christ and into a community of believers, baptism offers a compass through the rough terrain of various roles and identities. In terms of sexuality, baptism makes Christ's body the body of reference.

Baptism joins Christians to the body of Christ, a language so familiar its significance gets watered down. Baptism needs to be represented more vividly as a form of physical union, with all the attendant messiness but also with the whisper of ecstasy. At an Easter Vigil in a large urban Roman Catholic parish, thirty people of all ages were baptized into the body of Christ. The ceremony featured full immersion in a cattle trough, and the new Christians stumbled out of the trough with water streaming off them. They toweled off and left to change into dry clothes. After the first few baptisms, the chancel looked like the site of a brief, violent thunderstorm. But the ceremony proceeded, with the sponsors mopping up and the congregation singing out. The thirty returned, dried and freshly clothed, to be slathered with oil. Usually celebrants anoint using the oil sparingly and tracing only a tiny cross onto the forehead of the newly baptized. Not so in this service. The priests dipped their hands into bowls of scented oil and smeared it on the foreheads of these new Christians. Then they held the faces of the baptized in their hands and blessed them. Talk about fluids! Talk about mess!

The sensuality of the ceremony should not be surprising. Discipleship is all about bodies. In baptism Christians are incorporated into the body of Christ; in the Lord's Supper we receive Christ's body into our own as food and drink. When we take seriously the erotic dimension of these simple practices of discipleship, it is easy to see why people like the authors of Hosea and the Song of Solomon found in sexuality a metaphor for the life of faith. Bodies matter, and Christ's body matters most!

In defining our primary identity in terms of baptism, Christians move their primary loyalties out of the realm of biological family and into the realm of discipleship. Accordingly, we move sexuality from the private sphere into the public sphere. We acknowledge that who we are in body, mind, soul, and spirit is a public matter. With incorporation into the body of Christ, we confess that what we do in and with our bodies affects the body of Christ.

A prominent theologian declares that Christians are only interested in "sex in public"! He intends to be shocking, but he's not wrong. His words underscore the radical nature of a sexuality shaped by baptism. Adopting language from the legal realm, North American culture regards sexuality as a private matter. Laws regulating pornography, sodomy, abortion, and divorce have been wiped off the books in the name of "privacy." These laws discriminated against some classes of people while letting others enjoy fairly unlimited sexual privilege; yet they were eliminated on grounds of privacy rather than discrimination, and religious folk who should know better have adopted the line. Private sex is a fantasy. Almost everything that happens between two consenting adults affects others.

A friend from the locker room related a conversation that demonstrated powerfully how public her most intimate relationship was. My friend Sarah discovered that her daughter was a partner in her marriage. She related a conversation: "I don't even remember what started it. We hadn't even scheduled 'quality time'! But we got around to talking about marriage, and Chelsea said to me: 'Mom, I know you and Dad weren't always happy, but you stayed together and stuck it out. I'm so glad you did.'" As the woman spoke, it was clear that the shock of the words had not worn off. "I know I wasn't always the coolest mom. I'm not cool, and Richard's not cool. We were boring to her, both of us. Still, we were solid citizens, and I guess that counts for something. I never thought she had noticed."

A relationship between two consenting adults had repercussions the two adults had not counted on. Their daughter was clearly a partner in their marriage. Chelsea was deeply affected by another intimate relationship as well, and this marriage had not fared as well as her parents' had. The woman went on to say that Chelsea had been invited to read the journal of a good friend whose parents divorced when he was young. What he had written on his ninth birthday touched her deeply. His mother's general distraction left him feeling lonely and unworthy of her attention. "My daughter said, 'Mom, you never did that to me, and I feel so lucky.' What do you think of that? I'll have to tell Richard." These two solid citizens, Richard and my swimming buddy Sarah, may not have had the coolest or most romantic marriage, but their fidelity to one another profoundly impressed their daughter, a hidden partner in their marriage. In turn, the early divorce of another couple left a lasting impression on a young son. It also touched Sarah and Richard's daughter, a young girl in another family, making her grateful her parents had stayed together. These two teens stumbled on a truth that runs contrary to the myth that sex is a private matter. The cultural message that "what you do with your body is your own business" ought to be revised. Clearly what people do with their bodies has implications they cannot begin to imagine.

Far from being an act between two consenting adults, Christian sexuality is a crowded undertaking. What happens between two consenting adults affects a community. Think of how congregations treat people whose sexuality is suddenly on public display: a pregnant teenager in their midst, a divorced couple, a single person, a new widow or widower at a church gathering. Hopefully these folks encounter compassion rather than ostracism. Because we are baptized into the body of Christ, what happens with any of the bodies in our midst affects the whole. How do we tend the body? How can we re-member all people into the body of Christ?

The apostle Paul underscored this reality in writing to the pleasure-loving Corinthians. Some of them frequented prostitutes, and this concerned the apostle. Baptism plunged them into the body of Christ, and that bodily immersion into the waters of baptism had consequences. Baptism made sex a public matter, and Paul worried about the welfare of the body of Christ: "Do you not know that your bodies are members of Christ? Should I therefore take the members of Christ and make them members of a prostitute? Never! Do you not know that whoever is united to a prostitute becomes one body with her? For it is said, 'The two shall be one flesh.' But anyone united to the Lord becomes one spirit with him" (1 Corinthians 6:15–17). Paul knew that sexual activity affected the "one flesh" Christians shared in Christ. Here is a man who knows about sex in public.

The words of Paul to the Corinthians in the first century are echoed by words from Jim of Lake Wobegon in the twentieth. As Garrison Keillor narrates the story, Jim muses on the consequences of a trip to Chicago with a woman who is not his wife. Like Paul, he outlines the public dimension of sexuality:

> I sat there on the front lawn looking down the street. I saw that we all depend on each other. I saw that although I thought my sins would be secret, that they would be no more secret than an earthquake. All these houses and all these families—my infidelity will somehow shake them.

It will pollute the drinking water. It will make noxious gases come out of the ventilators in the elementary school. When we scream in senseless anger, blocks away a little girl we do not know spills a bowl of gravy all over a white tablecloth. If I go to Chicago with this woman who is not my wife, somehow the school patrol will forget to guard an intersection, and someone's child may be injured. A sixth-grade teacher will think, "What the hell!" and eliminate South America from geography. I just leave the story there. Anything more I could tell you would be self-serving. Except to say that we depend on each other more than we know.[2]

Jim contemplates adultery long enough to talk himself out of it.

The apostle Paul and the would-be adulterer Jim have in common the hard-won wisdom that what people do with their bodies matters not only to them but equally to their families and their communities. As Christians talk about sexuality, they discover an interdependence among the body of believers that demonstrates the public nature of sexuality.

## The Practice of Fidelity: Love Nurtured by Promises

A cartoon portrays two people at an altar reading their wedding vows. The caption reads, "As long as we both shall love." The cartoon is funny because although these vows are never spoken openly, they are implied. With around half of all marriages in the United States ending in divorce, love seems to be both rare and short-lived. The practice of fidelity allows love to flourish over time, in good seasons and in bad. The practice of fidelity emboldens couples to promise to be together "as long as we both shall live"—and mean it.

Some theologians speak of fidelity as a virtue because it points to constancy and perseverance that have become a habit. In calling it a practice, I stress that that fidelity also takes on flesh in daily and intentional expressions of faithfulness. It's great to engage in "random acts of kindness and spontaneous gifts of generosity," as bumper stickers urge. But fidelity goes beyond bumper stickers. It promises that these actions will not only be random and spontaneous but also steady and intentional. Expect them the way you count on the sun coming up each day.

My husband says to me playfully, "I'm sticking to you like green on grass." We laugh, and the laughter tides us both through the days when sticking with each other "like green on grass" is hard work. We obsess about work, surfacing from reading and writing only for meals. We travel in orbits far from one another, and home becomes a place to open mail, pay bills, and find clean clothes for the next trip. We struggle with very different strategies for relaxing: his involve throwing parties, food, and cooking, while mine tend toward road trips and travel. Daily we test our commitment to stick together. Daily we find the grace to honor that commitment. In addition to the infusion of daily graces, we practice fidelity, which demands steady and intentional acts of kindness, generosity, and plain old doggedness.

Are we natural romantics, my husband and I? Hardly. In fact, I seriously doubt that anyone can be a natural romantic for more than three days. Any relationship that hopes to last longer relies on the practice of fidelity. Fidelity commits to the fourth day—and beyond. Moral theologian Margaret Farley regards fidelity as "love's way of being whole while it still grows into wholeness."[3] Ceremonies of matrimony put it more simply: "I pledge thee my troth." Literally, the word *troth* meant "faithfulness." Faithfulness allows us to live with truthfulness because love promised brings out the truest self. In addition, promise-making and promise-keeping bring out the truest love. Love depends on promises made and promises kept in order for it to be love.

A group of high school youth explored the rich meaning of "pledging troth." A retreat featured a session on sexuality. The teens wrote out their questions about sex on a piece of paper, and then the papers were placed in a hat and shuffled, so no one knew which question came from whom. The hat was passed around, and everyone took out a question, read it aloud, and offered a few comments before inviting general discussion. After a few rounds, someone pulled out and read the following question: "How can I find true love?" Groans of mock exasperation opened to a thoughtful silence. This was the question no one wanted to ask but everyone wanted to have answered. After a long silence, someone ventured, "I guess that to find true love you have to find a true person." Another teen chimed in: "Don't you have to be a true person yourself? I mean, how am I going to be truthful with someone else if I can't tell myself the truth?" The teen knew something a lot of adults never figure out. There's no true love without truthful people. Promises create truthful people by returning them to the person they pledged to be. Promises made and promises kept create the rich soil for love; they sustain the practice of fidelity.

People find it difficult to guarantee today who they will be tomorrow. As a curb against basic human unpredictability, promises anchor people in a sea of possibilities. Promises tell us what we can do—and what we can't. Promises tell us who we are. An Irish activist priest working the Philippines spoke about how his vows grounded him: "I work with the pineapple workers' unions. Because I'm celibate, I can put myself on the picket lines and even be arrested, if it goes that far. If I had a wife and children at home, I'd have to be much more careful. And I can work closely with the women because we know just how far things will go—and how far they won't. Of course, I'd love to marry. But if I were married, I couldn't do the work I'm doing, and I love my work. In a way, my vows give me the freedom I need to do my work." Promises made and promises kept sustain this priest in his ministry. There may be struggle, but promises supply a compass in stormy weather. Publicly made and prayerfully tended promises help us keep faith.

Disciples need help keeping promises. Communities both enable and require people to make promises. No one is strong enough to keep the faith alone. People deliver on their promises in part because of other people's expectations but also because of other people's support. This is particularly true of promises made around sexual relationships. I remember dinner with friends only hours after my husband and I had had a heated argument. Our friends expected us to be the animated, loving couple we usually are. Gradually the warmth of their affection for us resurrected our deep affection for each other. These people loved us into being the people we'd promised to be. They welcomed us back into what Wendell Berry calls "the country of marriage,"[4] and promises are the passport into that gracious land.

Not everyone traverses the country of marriage, but the world according to God welcomes anyone. Promises welcome the one who enters. Baptism inducts Christians into a community created by promise. Parents and godparents promise to nurture a child in the faith; a community promises its support; both community and sponsors promise on behalf of a child or infant who may be too young to attend to the surrounding symphony of promises performed in its midst. At the heart of all of these promises are God's promises, drawing a Christian into the body of his Son, Jesus. These promises are the soil for a love that comes from Love itself.

If promises kept sustain love, promises broken cripple it, souring love into resentment, bitterness, even annihilation. The threat to fidelity is betrayal, and the disciple Judas embodies infidelity. Though he was guilty of no sexual sin, Judas' example speaks volumes about betrayal. His betrayal isolates him. He is ostracized by the community of disciples and by the religious authorities who paid him. Cut loose from the loves of his various communities, he cannot love himself. Words from scripture ring hauntingly true: "Woe to that one by whom the Son of Man is betrayed! It would have been better for that one not to have been born" (Matthew 26:24). Judas ends his own life, untrue to his Lord, to his community, and to himself.

Judas' story brings fresh insight to "true love" and the promises that sustain it. Betrayal hurts, but it hurts the betrayer as well. If the betrayal is known, as Judas' was, the betrayer loses the trust of those around him. Would you trust someone so inconstant? You might be next! Untruthful people find themselves alone, deprived of human contact that would make them whole. If the betrayal is not known, the betrayer walls himself away in his own guilt and self-hatred. The Australian movie *Lantana* offers a stunning cameo of infidelity. As the movie unfolds, a highly intuitive detective investigates the death of a prominent author. He senses that many of the prime suspects are guilty, but he misreads their betrayals because he himself is guilty. He has embarked on an affair that could end his marriage, and he projects his own guilt on everyone around him. His miscalculations mount along with his sense of betrayal, and the detective catches a glimpse of the man he will become if he continues his affair. Even if he can continue to keep it hidden, he realizes that his adultery will turn him into someone he despises. He ends the affair. Eventually the detective confesses everything to his wife, hoping that the strength of their love exceeds the afternoon of his infidelity. His wife receives the revelation with cold anger: "It's easy to find someone else," she lashes out, "the hard thing is not to." But over time they reconcile, as together they place his infidelity into their past. The movie shows a good man and a good woman struggling to stay good. That means keeping faith, even in the face of betrayal and promises broken.

As a practice of discipleship, fidelity seems somewhat elusive. In their indexes and tables of contents, books of worship list no rituals for fidelity. If they did, the prayers for repairing broken promises might be the most well-thumbed part of the prayer book. Yet fidelity stands at the heart of the biblical witness, as it delineates the ethics of a God whose promises litter the Bible. This God promises with a rainbow not to destroy the world again, promises with an heir to make a childless couple the father and mother of nations, promises with the child of a young Jewish mother to save the whole of creation. These are not "just promises," empty words spoken with good intent and no follow-through. Divine promises come true in the body of Christ, sent into the world to deliver on God's promises.

Christ is the good faith of God, and baptism makes disciples a part of that body. Disciples live out the ethics of this faithful God, and the promises of baptism shape the lifestyle of discipleship, nowhere more powerfully than in our exercise of sexuality.

## The Sexual Ethics of Discipleship: Relationships to God, Self, and Others

A young priest lamented, "The fact that I'm not married doesn't mean I'm not sexual or somehow asexual. It means I exercise the sexuality appropriate to my calling as a priest. For me, that's celibacy." This young man suggests that different callings demand different kinds of sexual accountability. His calling as a priest requires celibacy. Another calling to be married or partnered, single or widowed, would require a different kind of sexual accountability. Traditionally the word *chastity* was used to describe sexual accountability. Chastity depended on the disciple's calling; it ruled out some actions to enable other goods to flourish. For example, for the sake of intimacy, chastity in marriage ruled out a range of actions that compromised it: marital rape, abuse, adultery, domestic violence, or withholding sex. For the freedom to love a wide range of people, chastity in the priesthood ruled out focused sexual involvement, which compromised a priest's ability to be emotionally accessible to everyone in his care. When the apostle Paul counseled his beloved Corinthians to "Be chaste!" he was not necessarily signing them up for abstinence. Rather he reminded them that as part of the body of Christ (1 Corinthians 5:13 ff.), they were to be sexually accountable to that body. When Paul cautioned the Corinthians to be chaste, the message he delivered was more like "Act responsibly!" than "Don't touch!" Unfortunately, the rich meanings embedded in chastity have been lost, and the term is today commonly confused with celibacy and sexual abstinence.

A Christian sexual ethics that draws on a first language of faith resurrects some of the wisdom chastity intended. Such ethics might advise a young priest, a married or partnered couple, an elderly man or woman, a teen. People who claim the lifestyle of discipleship find their primary identity in baptism, their fundamental orientation to the body of Christ, and their sexual practice informed by fidelity and safeguarded by promises.

A sexual ethics of discipleship begins with an identity that we all share, because it begins with a body we are all a part of. Perhaps before we begin talking sex, we should return to the font, plunging our bodies into the waters of baptism. Consider this to be God's part in the conversation. Inviting God's participation in Christian sexual ethics demands careful attention to scripture.

As a teaching theologian of the church, I get questions about what scripture says regarding divorce and remarriage, the new genetic technologies, weapons of mass destruction, homo- and heterosexuality. In my darker moments, I have come to regard this as the hermeneutics of narcissism: "What does the Bible say about *me me me!*" If we turn to the Bible only for advice on *our* conduct, we miss the story it tells us about God. As it unfolds in dazzling detail, scripture narrates the ethics of God: the mystery of creation and fall; the life, death, and resurrection of Jesus Christ; the Spirit who persistently bears us up—often in spite of ourselves. When we look at this key source of moral deliberation as a narration of the ethics of God, it yields fresh insight. It tells us a lot about the One to whom we belong and what our response should be to that membership.

The apostle Paul thought a lot about belonging in the body of Christ. He talked about sex all over the ancient world to vastly different communities with dizzyingly different practices. In the midst of such diversity, Paul focused on Christ's body as the common body of belonging. He did not always tell people what to do, but he was quite clear on what God had done for them in Christ Jesus. He framed Christian identity as a matter of baptismal belonging: "You belong to Christ, and Christ belongs to God" (1 Corinthians 3:23). If Paul is right, the ethics of God has a lot to say about sexuality: it tells us *who* we are by telling us *whose* we are.

What should our response be as members of the body of Christ? Simply this: love. Love of God shapes how we love ourselves and how we love each other. The Great Commandment is not usually cited when Christians talk about sex: "You shall love the Lord your God with all your heart, and with all your soul, and with all your strength, and with all your mind; and your neighbor as your self" (Luke 10:27–28; compare Matthew 22:36–40; Mark 12:28–34; Deuteronomy 6:5; Leviticus 19:18). Perhaps the ethics of narcissism is to blame: "This text doesn't tell *me* what to do with *my* body in *my* sexual relationships!" Too bad! The Great Commandment tells us about God—the ethics of God—and tells us how to belong to God. It details three important relationships at stake in any Christian sexual ethics: a relationship to God, a relationship to self, and a relationship to another person. A sexual ethics of discipleship treats dimensions of prayer, power, and the various parts of the human person.

### "You Shall Love the Lord Your God": Relationship to God and the Dimension of Prayer

"You shall love the Lord your God." An extravagant love of God is the starting point for a sexual ethics of discipleship. The danger of idolatry simmers below the surface of sexuality. As news of the Roman Catholic sex scandals leaked into the press, a common confusion emerged. "I thought he was God; after all, he was my priest," said one adult abused as a child. Priests preyed on the confusion; parents reinforced it. The temptation to play God feeds predation.

A culture that places priests and pastors on a pedestal plays accomplice to these scandals. This can be quite seductive to men and women of the cloth. As one clergywoman confessed, "People think you are a lot holier than you are, and it's hard not to believe that. My parishioners credit me with a lot more power than I have—or should have. It's seductive. I fight it all the time." The Great Commandment calls for an end to all idolatry, whether fueled by internal narcissism or external need. In demanding a primary relationship to God, the Great Commandment reminds disciples to be loving *disciples*, not masters in training. Let God be God.

This counsel plays out among couples as well, where the temptation is strong to play God or let the other take the role. These twin idolatries erase self and other as bounded and distinct subjects. They thrust God from the relationship. Because he has seen the wages of idolatry so often, a pastor puts the same line in every wedding sermon: "And so the two shall become one. The question is, which one?" The line always catches people off guard; they laugh nervously. This pastor has seen too many relationships collapse because one person gradually gets lost in the other. Initially the sacrifice that such enmeshment demands is offered generously and with enthusiasm. How often we've heard someone gush, "I would do anything for him!" However, over time what started in emotion becomes erasure. "I felt like one of the figures in my kids' coloring books, only the thick black lines around me had begun to blur. You didn't know where to color anymore," a harried wife and mother muses. She risks becoming resentful and rising up years later to claim a life she feels she's lost. Meanwhile the other partner may be feeling boredom or claustrophobia, neither one a good atmosphere for intimacy.

Probably no advice columnist can save a relationship that has slowly imploded, but a healthy spirituality at the outset can curb idolatry. It gives the couple a center of gravity outside either one of them; it gives each an identity outside the relationship. A healthy spirituality highlights the importance of a common religious belief, common spiritual practices, or at least a common sense of the holy. This may not seem important in the early stages of a relationship, when being head over heels in love creates a momentum that seems like it could last forever. Any relationship headed for the long haul, however, will weather its share of joys and sorrows. No one can play God for very long, whether he seeks the role or finds it foisted on him.

Long-term couples seek comfort in a center outside themselves. A middle-aged Hawaiian woman gave utterance to this need. She'd long been married to a Buddhist, a mixed marriage that was not uncommon in that culturally diverse state: "We respect one another's beliefs, but it was hard for the children. We raised them Catholic because my family insisted on it. But the children didn't understand why, if my Catholicism was so important to me, their father wasn't a part of it as well. And now that they have grown up and gone away, it's hard for me. I miss sharing a common spirituality." A minister who does a lot of premarital counseling in a denomination that discourages premarital cohabitation finds prayer more intimate than sex. "I ask couples if they are living together," she says, "because living together is so different from being married. But the hardest question I ask is whether they can pray together. They get kind of embarrassed." Couples who work toward a common spirituality will find a center outside themselves, a curb against idolatry and implosion.

## "With All Your Heart and Soul and Mind and Strength": Relationship to Self and the Various Parts of the Human Person

The Great Commandment describes a complex unity of many parts: heart, soul, mind, and strength. What happens with the body sends shock waves throughout the human person. Some people may talk about sexuality as a "gift," but in fact it is often a powder keg. Sexuality is volatile because it renders us so utterly vulnerable. We stand utterly exposed before one another.

Physical nakedness is not the problem: we manage that in locker rooms with minimal embarrassment. Rather the other kinds of nakedness—emotional, spiritual, even intellectual—threaten to light a fuse that could blow everything sky high. Ah! the psalmist was right: we are "fearfully and wonderfully made" (Psalms 139:14). Good sex bestows ecstasy; bad sex can blow us up. Survivors of

abuse learn to stay fragmented because they cannot bear to remember. One survivor remembers watching her uncle molest her from
somewhere else in the room. She willed herself to have an out-of-
body experience because it was too painful to inhabit the body she
was in. Only after years of therapy could she reconnect to herself—
literally, re-member herself—body, mind, soul, and spirit.

We are created in the image of a passionate God, a God who loves
our various parts into a unique and wondrous whole. "Our heart is
restless until it rests in you," wrote Augustine of Hippo fifteen centuries ago. The book that opens with this line concludes with an
exploration of how God fills the five senses and permeates memory,
intellect, and desire.[5] Augustine's God seduces him body, soul, mind,
and spirit. Reading this tale of seduction, we long to love and be
loved as he was. Augustine found peace in a loving God—and not
just peace but integrity. God's love embraces us in the wholeness of
our various parts, and it reminds us to respect that integrity.

Sexual accountability that honors the integrity of the human person is particularly tricky for adolescents and teens, for whom some
parts develop more quickly than others. I watch my teenage nieces
moon around the house. I know they are not thinking about the
stock market. One minute they are children, playing with their dolls;
the next they are adults, vamping in short skirts and bikinis. When
they look up from their Barbies, they notice that boys are noticing
them. Emotional maturity lags far behind physical maturity in these
girl-women. They are truly "fearfully and wonderfully" made, and
I pray that they will not be preyed on, that their sexual encounters will not disrupt a developing integrity of body, mind, soul,
and spirit.

### "And You Shall Love Your Neighbor as Yourself": Relationship to Other People and the Dimension of Power

Our relationship to a passionate God has implications for our relationship to "the other." The other is the neighbor; the other bears
the face of Christ our Brother. Regarding the face of Christ in the

face of our partner presents the other, not as slave or master or parent, but as equal, as brother or sister in Christ. Regarding the other as an equal brings the dimension of power into the issue of sexual accountability.

Relationships of perfect equality are probably an illusion. If they did exist, they would prove boring. The question is not whether there are imbalances in a union but rather how they are known, named, and negotiated. "Our relationship is never fifty-fifty," said a busy father and investment banker. "Sometimes it's eighty-twenty; sometimes it's twenty-eighty. And then there are the times it's eighty-eighty. I like knowing that she'll spell me, if something comes up. And I cover the home front when she's got a big project. We try to pay attention."

A lot of sexual misconduct represents fundamentally an abuse of power. Someone with more power, by virtue of age or status or gender or privilege, coerces someone into sexual activity that the other person does not want or is unable to consent to freely. Instances of pedophilia (adult sexual contact with children) or ephebophilia (adult sexual contact with adolescents) involve coercive sexual conduct. While the minor may not have objected at the time, the situation itself was coercive because adults hold the power of age and experience over children.

Sometimes abuse of power is blatant, as when an employer demands sexual favors from an employee. Sometimes abuse of power is more subtle. A young woman involved with her grad school professor swore up and down that she was "a consenting adult," refusing to understand that she was not free to consent to be in a relationship with someone who would evaluate her dissertation, write recommendations for her, and find a job for her. Attending to power differentials in a relationship contributes to a sense of sexual accountability.

Finally, a sexual ethics that begins with baptism can dare to speak about sexuality positively. Sexual ethics moves from being a containment policy or a rehearsal of "thou shalt nots" to a positive platform for service to God and neighbor. If we are members of the body of Christ, sex ought to do some good for the world Christ came to save.

## Conclusion: Not Just Good Sex but Positive Sex

Whatever the disciple's sexual commitment, Christian sexuality ought to be directed by positive norms of faithfulness, generativity, and service.

Faithfulness among disciples imitates the faithfulness of God in Christ. After all, Jesus didn't discard the disciples because of their complaining, cluelessness, and towering disloyalty. He stuck with them, leaving them and us an incarnate example of faithfulness.

Generativity demands that Christians "pay back" the good gifts they have received by "paying forward" something to the next generation. Some will contribute children and grandchildren; others will teach and tutor. In signaling an obligation to the future, generativity embodies hope.

Finally, we make jokes about "sexual services," but service ought to be a part of sexuality. People committed to religious life focus their sexuality on service, as the Irish priest said: "Because I'm celibate, I can put myself on the picket lines, get arrested, if it comes to that. If I had a wife and children at home, I'd have to be far more cautious." By the same token, marriage does not grant a couple permission to form their own hermetically sealed dyad. Rather it invites them to serve the neighbor and to be a neighbor to those in need. My colleague builds houses for Habitat for Humanity one Saturday a month. His wife does not join him, but "I leave her with all the Saturday chores that day. That's her contribution: it makes it possible for me to be here hammering away." The two work in different parts of the vineyard, joined by a common commitment to serve. Faithfulness, generativity, and service: if Christians draw on their first language of faith, they can find some positive things to say about sexuality. The sexual ethics of discipleship does not degenerate to a list of "thou shalt nots" but rather moves into a world according to God.

My fear is that Christians move uncritically in the worlds of legal briefs and glossy magazines, editorial magazines and talk shows. They discuss sexual identity as if it were a person's sole center of gravity. They define sexual orientation in terms of the gender of the people to whom one is usually attracted. They discuss sexual behavior negatively as a list of "thou shalt nots," as if there were nothing positive to say. They speak of sexual practice as a kind of containment policy: what not to do with what to whom. They act as if the choice between "homosexuality" and "heterosexuality" were the only lifestyle choices around. This is not the way Christians should be talking about sexuality.

In a world according to God, Christian talk about sex should begin not in the bedroom but at the baptismal font. We need to resurrect our first language of faith when we talk about sex. Fidelity is the practice of discipleship that safeguards sexuality; promises are the mechanism that secure it. Our primary identity is that we are Christians; our primary orientation is to the body of Christ; our primary behavior is defined by baptism. If we begin at the font, we will discover a common calling to the lifestyle of discipleship.

# 9

............................................

# Practicing Resurrection

My parents were avid gardeners and spent every Saturday they could in the yard, pruning and planting, mowing and weeding. At the end of the day, they would sit on the porch and take pleasure in what they had done. No doubt the Creator did this at the end of each day of creation, and the book of Genesis packs it into a terse benediction: "And God saw that it was good."

My sister and I worked to avoid these adventures in the garden. Our joint strategy was to keep our heads down, pleading homework or sewing projects—anything that would keep us inside the house. But we joined our parents at the end of the day for their ritual rest. As one of these Saturdays drew to a close, we all watched as the cat tried to snag a bird from the lowest branch of the birch tree. The bird seemed aware of the situation, staying well out of harm's way but close enough to taunt the cat. We children wanted to take the cat inside, but my father overruled us: "Cats chase birds; that's just what they do. Relax: let the cat be a cat."

My father knew what it meant to be a cat. At the time, his knowledge impressed me deeply. It probably sent me on a lifelong quest to sift the essences of things. Like the cat straining to jump high enough to reach the bird, everything in this book strains to address the question, What does it mean to be a disciple? The nature of a cat is to track birds; the nature of a disciple is to follow Jesus.

The first chapter in this book takes its bearings on discipleship from Gospel stories of the earthly Jesus and his first disciples, particularly Peter. Jesus called all of them with the words "Follow me." They followed, finding Jesus so attractive that they left everything to be with him. It was not the journey they expected, nor was Jesus the master they thought he would be. Yet the disciples kept following, and Jesus did not abandon them. Finally, he introduced Peter and the rest to a world beyond their wildest imagination: a world according to God.

This final chapter takes its bearings on discipleship from the resurrected Christ and the last words he spoke to Peter: "Follow me." In following Jesus, the original disciples thought they would find freedom from Roman occupation, from oppressive and expensive purity codes, from poverty and want. Jesus led them to resurrection instead. Resurrection was as radical a concept then as it is now. The practices Jesus left behind invite us into a zone of resurrection. Poet Wendell Berry hints at how different life looks from the vantage of resurrection: "Practice resurrection."[1]

What does it mean to practice resurrection? Practicing resurrection begins with the core practices of discipleship: baptism, the Lord's Supper, prayer, forgiveness, remembering the dead, and fidelity. As long as they have confessed "Jesus is Lord," Christians have done these things in memory of the One whom we loved and followed. As we practice, we become what we confess: the body of Christ in the world. The practices that the risen Christ left behind mark a zone of resurrection in a world that strains for it. These practices makes disciples "marked" men and women; they offer a glimpse of the world from a God's-eye view.

## Life in the Resurrection Zone

The events between Good Friday and the descent of the Holy Spirit at Pentecost constitute Jesus' last parable. He does not put this parable into words; he puts it into practices. Perhaps Jesus finally

understood the disciples' constant complaining about how confusing his parables were to them. This time he puts his parable into
actions, leaving the disciples with a series of practices that would
help disciples follow him when he was gone.

One of them, Saint Francis of Assisi, who lived in the thirteenth
century, helps us understand Jesus' last parable. He was a renowned
preacher, but he did not always deliver his sermons from pulpits, nor
did he put them in words. He preached the Gospel in everything
he did. In his interactions with the poor and outcast, in his great
delight over the spectrum of God's creation, even in his gentle teasing about human failings, Francis radiated the Good News. "Preach
the Gospel without ceasing," he is reported to have said. "Use words
if necessary."

The lectionary for the days between Good Friday and Pentecost
chronicles the events that became Jesus' last parable. On Good
Friday, the disciples faced overwhelming loss. They grieved the
death of their beloved friend Jesus. This was real death, the end of
life as they knew it. Easter was the beginning of new life, life as they
could barely imagine it. Easter brought with it resurrection, but resurrection did not resuscitate Jesus or return the disciples to life as
they had known it. Resurrection created life on new terms
entirely—life in the Resurrection Zone.

The resurrection was like an earthquake, and the earliest disciples struggled to find their own post-Easter bearings. When the
ground stopped shaking, they found the landscape dramatically
altered. They were frightened about being identified as Jesus' disciples. They locked themselves in upper rooms. They reverted
to familiar occupations: fishing, teaching, drifting. After Easter,
the disciples did whatever they could to keep the ground from
moving again.

Despite all of the disciples' best efforts to escape it, resurrection
found them. The risen Christ searched them out. He moved
through locked doors into closed rooms, offering them peace. He
joined them as they fled to Emmaus, unlocking the secrets of the

scriptures. He even found them on a beach as they fished—and cooked them breakfast. The risen Christ searched them out, and he searches us out. Disciples cannot escape resurrection.

This is not necessarily good news. The disciples desperately wanted to bolt from the Easter proclamation: "Christ is risen. Christ is risen indeed!" The Gospel accounts of the resurrection feature a lot of running. The bereaved disciples raced around like competition sprinters. Standing still in the face of resurrection required more courage than anyone could seem to muster. The disciples wanted the old Jesus back again; instead, they keep running into the risen Christ. They did not recognize the risen Christ, nor did they always welcome him. The resurrected Christ found them nonetheless.

It was no easier when the disciples stood still. At the empty tomb, Mary Magdalene wept to have her old friend back again. She reached out to touch Jesus—and he wouldn't let her (John 20:17). Gently but firmly, Jesus forced Mary Magdalene to adjust to life in the Resurrection Zone. The apostle Thomas refused to believe unless he could touch Jesus' crucified body. This time Jesus obliged, but with a scold and a challenge: "Blessed are those who have not seen and yet have come to believe" (John 20:29). The risen Christ said to the disciples—and to all of us, "Get used to life in the Resurrection Zone." Both Mary Magdalene and Thomas wanted what they had before, the familiar Jesus, the comfortable Jesus, the "old shoe" Jesus. In the back of my mind, I hear the voice of my mother lamenting her painful arthritic feet. "I don't want new shoes," she protested. "I want my old shoes back again." Resurrection never gives back our old shoes. Resurrection gives us new feet. The problem is that we now need to learn to walk all over again.

The risen Christ helped the disciples take their first steps. He gave them time to adjust to life in the Resurrection Zone. The forty days between Easter and Ascension defer to the disciples' longing to have the old Jesus back again. The forty days were God's

concession to the human need for a comfort zone, a space of adjust-
ment. The forty days gave the disciples time to reorient their lives to
life in the Resurrection Zone.

I remember coming out of a movie theater into the bright light
of an afternoon sun. For a moment I ducked back into the darkness,
because the late afternoon light dazzled my eyes. I stepped into the
shade until my pupils adjusted. How much brighter is resurrection—
and how great the temptation to choose darkness over that great
light. The risen Christ made allowance for the disciples' eyes to
adjust. Once again, Jesus did not abandon his disciples. He gave
them time to recognize their former teacher in the risen Christ. He
stuck around to reassure them, to cook for them, to teach them
again. The disciples got a chance to grieve their loss and get used
to life in the Resurrection Zone.

When Jesus ascends into heaven, the disciples let go. The great
German Reformation artist Albrecht Dürer depicted the Ascension
in a woodcut. The picture focuses on the disciples, who stand in dis-
array staring at two feet dangling out of a great cloud at the top of
the cut. The rest of Jesus has ascended beyond the frame. Some
of the disciples try to grab Jesus by the feet and pull him back down
to earth; others try to grab onto his robe and hitch a ride into the
heavens. True to the account of the Ascension in the Book of Acts,
there are two angels in the midst of the disciples, and we know from
the Ascension story in the Book of Acts what they are saying: "Men
of Galilee, why do you stand looking into heaven?" (Acts 1:11).
The angels' words register as a rebuke: "Why do you stand looking
into heaven? Don't long for what is no longer with you. Don't waste
your time longing for the old Jesus. Attend to what is here. Your
ministry lies here, on earth, among your neighbors. Practice
resurrection."

The time between Easter and Ascension has prepared the disciples to see Jesus return to his Father. Perhaps the hands reaching
out for Jesus' robe are hands that have just released Jesus from his
earthly home, released him like a child letting go of a helium

balloon. With the Ascension, the disciples let go, relinquishing the old. With the Ascension, the disciples let this great loss bless them.[2]

Let us cling for a moment to this piece of Jesus' last parable: letting your loss bless you. It's the practice that the risen Christ leaves behind when he ascends into heaven. We reenact Jesus' Ascension when we remember our dead, acknowledging how important they are and were to us yet allowing them to leave us. I remember speaking with a friend who lost a husband and life partner suddenly and cruelly. She worked through her grief and anger to a point where she said, "I could finally see how, if this had to happen, it had happened in the most gracious way possible. We'd made love in the morning, pruned our roses after breakfast, and then parted with a kiss. Things that were not usually in place were in place on that day." This woman had internalized Jesus' last parable. She found its resonance in her own life. She stopped clinging to her sorrow and anguish. She was ready to let go. She was letting her loss bless her.

Perhaps the disciples did the same as they watched Jesus ascend into the heavens. They had forty days between Easter and Ascension to adjust to life in the Resurrection Zone. As they got used to the absence of Jesus, the disciples found the grace to let their loss bless them. Life without Jesus to teach them, frustrate them, and drag them around the Galilean countryside meant a whole new life. There was no point in longing for the old life. The old life had left them behind, and the call to ministry lay ahead.

The disciples were not left comfortless; they received resources to answer their callings. The risen Christ promised he would send his Spirit, and he honored that promise. With Pentecost, the Spirit of God in Jesus Christ descends on the disciples with tongues of fire. An old English psalter depicted this graphically. In one of the colorful illustrations for this volume, a fire-breathing dove, its head in a halo, descends from the heavens. Flames from its mouth alight on the heads of the assembled crowd. Eyes wide, the disciples point to the tongues of fire on the heads of the others. It may be that the flames singed their hair as they fanned their spirits, but from that moment on, they live as marked men and women, people of the Resurrection Zone.

## Marks of the Spirit, Practices of Resurrection

Before he died in 1226, Saint Francis spent a night in fasting and prayer on the top of Mount La Verna. There the crucified Christ appeared to him, bright with light and borne on angels' wings. As Francis rose from prayer to embrace his risen Lord, he received in his own flesh the wounds of Christ, the *stigmata*. From that night forward, Francis was a marked man.

The story captured the imagination of medieval artists, who widely depicted Francis' night of fasting and prayer in paintings, frescoes, and finely wrought miniatures. The sheer number of images makes clear that the stigmatization of Francis fascinated medieval Christians, who looked for some badge or bodily symbol of belonging to the body of Christ.

The story of Francis holds a mirror to our own time. As we look through the window of Christian history to marvel at Francis' piety, we catch a glimpse of ourselves looking. The stigmatization of Francis confronts us with our own desire to be marked. It manifests itself in piercings, tattoos, hair colors not easily found in nature. Even though I wince at the multiple piercings in the checkout clerk's ears and stare at the stud in a student's tongue, I understand the desire to be marked. In a culture that seems ephemeral and transient, bodily markings give people something no one else can take away. Identity and belonging: these markings tell us who and whose we are.

What images today move people to mark their own bodies, just as images of Francis' stigmatization shaped important strands of medieval spirituality? In these times we watched the World Trade Center towers fall; we saw footage of the carnage in the Middle East. We counted body bags from wars in Afghanistan and Iraq. We agonized over the efforts of forensic teams to identify body parts and corpses, and we feared they would find someone we knew. Is it not surprising that we too want to be marked so that people will know who we are? The need to be marked does not seem antiquated or obsolete. People long for a center of gravity, and many claim it in their own bodies.

Christians find their center of gravity in the body of Christ. At the time of his death, Christ's body was marked. It bore the marks of nails in his hands and his feet; a sword pierced his chest. When resurrection altered everything else, these marks identified the risen Christ as the crucified Jesus of Nazareth. The apostle Thomas would not believe that he was in the presence of old Jesus until he could see and touch these marks in the body of the risen Christ.

Twenty-first-century disciples are not expected to do much better. We have not traveled the dusty roads of ancient Galilee, nor can we boast of the sanctity of Francis. We too need to put our hands into the marks of the body of Christ to know that we are in the presence of the Lord. That reassurance is given in a series of resurrection practices. Where people are doing these acts, there is the body of Christ. Baptizing and catechizing new members, breaking bread and drinking wine, fumbling toward forgiveness, waiting to be enveloped by prayer: these simple acts identify us to ourselves and to others.

We need reminding who we are. My friend Nancy went to visit her grandmother in the nursing home where she was confined with Alzheimer's disease. The older woman was quite convinced that her residence was a shop that she owned, and she bossed around the other residents with great gusto. At the end of her visit, Nancy stopped at a hallway mirror to take a picture of herself and her grandmother with her Polaroid. A few minutes later, the photo was developed. The two of them studied it closely in silence, and then Nancy's grandmother piped up: "Well, I look pretty good. But who's the old lady?" She thought she was her granddaughter. The older woman was lost in some part of her earlier life. She could not recognize herself as she was. Of course, my friend had no inclination to find her and to resituate her in the present. Better that she stay lost.

People get lost all the time—and few have the excuse of a cruel and irreversible disease. Work, families, jobs, and the demands of leisure leave people lost and uncertain of the way forward. "I just feel off-center," one of my colleagues confessed. "Maybe it's menopause." We studied her appointment book. It wasn't just menopause: she had spent seven out of the last eight weekends on the road. She had had no time to regroup. A weekend in familiar surroundings would ground her again.

Spiritual dislocation registers more subtly. "I once was lost but now am found"—the well-loved words speak of being spiritually off-center. Disciples who want to be found rely on the compass of practices that have oriented Christians for centuries. These identify us to ourselves. My husband was talking with one of his college students. When a young woman proposed going to the beach instead of going to Mass, her boyfriend declined. "That's just who I am," he said without apology. "And church is where you find me on Sunday mornings." Church was where she could find him, because church was where the young man found himself. The ritual of Sunday worship organized his week; the rhythm of the liturgy oriented his soul.

Several years ago, a month of delegations and conferences took my husband and me in quick succession from Oakland, California, to war-torn Guatemala, then on to Florence, Italy, and Stuttgart, Germany, before returning to our home. Each Sunday, we attended Mass in the local Roman Catholic parish. Whether in the highlands of Guatemala or the medieval splendor of the Duomo in Florence or a parish church in rural Germany, the shape of the Mass was the same. We followed along, whether we understood all the words or not. In the midst of great beauty and great suffering, the familiar rhythm of the liturgy oriented us to a God "whose beauty is past change."[3] We found a center of gravity in the rhythm of prayer and praise, a home base in the midst of our travels.

Resurrection practices make Christ present in a world that longs to see his face. They serve as the post-Easter incarnation, and this incarnational logic rolls out like the familiar Taize chant: *Ubi caritas et amor, ibi deus est*, "Where you find charity and love, there you find God." Like a compass needle that swings to the north, resurrection practices locate the body of Christ in the world. Wherever you find people baptizing, there you find the body of Christ in the world. Wherever you find people breaking bread together in the name of Jesus, there you find the body of Christ. Wherever you find people praying, there you find the body of Christ. Wherever you find people forgiving and being forgiven, there you find the body. Wherever you find people honoring their dead in memory of the one who was raised from the dead, there you find the body. Wherever you find people making and keeping promises in imitation of an ever-faithful God, there you find the body.

Many Christians count these core practices as acts of worship, and they are surely directed toward God as the giver of all good things. But these resurrection practices also identify Christians to others and locate the body of Christ in the world. Simply put, they testify. As Christians practice resurrection, they become the body of Christ in the world. Indeed, they may be the only way others encounter Christ's body in the world.

## Remembering the World According to God

Participating in the practices he left behind, disciples remember their risen Lord and act at his command. When Jesus broke bread and drank wine with the disciples in their final meal together, he asked them to "do this in remembrance of me" (Luke 22:19). *Memory* in the Resurrection Zone is a loaded term; it bears two powerful definitions. On the one hand, *memory* means literally calling to mind again and again. As we have seen in the practice of prayer, remembering entails paying attention. A young mother tells her child, "Mind me!" and she invokes the first sense of memory. "Remember what I told you about that playing with your cousins." As the voice of the mother gets internalized, the child no longer needs prompting. He discovers the ability to "mind" his mother, even when she is absent.

The apostle Paul reached for this quality of mind and heart when he entreated the community at Philippi to "mind" Christ: "Let the same mind be in you that was in Christ Jesus" (Philippians 2:5). He asked them to hear the voice of Christ, even when it was not spoken. Internalizing the mind of Christ, the Philippians would inhabit it as their own. They would see things as Christ did: the world according to God.

On the other hand, when Jesus charged the disciples to "do this in remembrance of me," he pointed to a second sense of *memory*. He signaled that the practice of sharing in his body and blood literally re-members his body in the world. Doing this "in remembrance of me" resurrects his body, making Christ present once again. Practicing resurrection re-presents the body of Christ in a world that, like the apostle Thomas, longs to touch him. As members of the body of Christ, we re-member that body in the world.

## A World According to God

If discipleship is all about following, where do disciples find Jesus today? We meet him where he promised to be: in the resurrection practices that he left behind. Surely this is not the only place where Jesus meets us, but if we learn to find him here, we will recognize him elsewhere. My father's roses were not the only roses in the world, but I learned to recognize roses from his garden, kind and color and species. I also learned how to tell them from the weeds. As we break bread and drink wine in memory of Jesus' final meal, as we baptize in the name of the Triune God, as we pray the prayer Jesus taught us to pray, as we forgive and ask for forgiveness, as we honor the dead, and as we live out the promises we make, we remember who Jesus is—so that we can find him elsewhere. More important, through these practices we become his body in the world so that others too may follow.

# Notes

## Chapter One: Imagining a World According to God

1. Annie Dillard, Holy the Firm (New York: HarperCollins, 1977), p. 59.

2. Marcus Borg, Meeting Jesus Again for the First Time (San Francisco: HarperSanFrancisco, 1994).

3. Gerard Manley Hopkins, "As Kingfishers Catch Fire, Dragonflies Draw Flame," in Poetry and Prose (London: Everyman Paperbacks, 1998), p. 70.

4. I owe much to Dorothy Bass and the groundbreaking work she has done on practices: see Dorothy C. Bass (ed.), Practicing Our Faith (San Francisco: Jossey-Bass, 1997). (In Practicing Our Faith, Bass define practices as "shared activities that address fundamental human needs and that, woven together, form a way of life" [p. xi]. I want to identify that "way of life" more explicitly as a life of discipleship). Cf. Miroslav Volf and Dorothy C. Bass (eds.), Practicing Theology: Beliefs and Practices in Christian Life (Grand Rapids, Mich.: Eerdmans, 2002); and Dorothy C. Bass, Receiving the Day: Christian Practices for Opening the Gift of Time (San Francisco: Jossey-Bass, 2000).

5. Roberta Bondi, "Praying the Lord's Prayer: Truthfulness, Intercessory Prayer, and Formation in Love," in E. Byron Anderson and Bruce T. Morrill (eds.), Liturgy and the Moral Self: Humanity at Full Stretch Before God (Collegeville, Minn.: Liturgical Press, 1998), p. 165.

6. Kathleen Norris, *The Cloister Walk* (New York: Riverhead Books, 1987), p. 6.

7. Iris Murdoch, *The Sovereignty of Good* (New York: Routledge, 1970), p. 37.

## Chapter Three: Baptism: Joining the Journey

1. Dietrich Bonhoeffer, *Life Together/Prayerbook of the Bible* (Minneapolis: Fortress Press, 1996), p. 44.

## Chapter Five: Prayer: Conversations Along the Way

1. Simone Weil, *Waiting for God,* trans. Emma Craufurd (San Francisco: HarperSanFrancisco, 1951), p. 113.

2. Ibid., p. 124. Weil identifies three elements in affliction: physical pain, social alienation, and the threat of spiritual abandonment.

3. Martin Luther, "Comfort for Women Who Have Had a Miscarriage," trans. James Raun, in Gustav K. Wiencke (ed.), *Luther's Works,* vol. 45 (Minneapolis: Fortress Press, 1968), pp. 243–250.

4. Dietrich Bonhoeffer, *Discipleship,* trans. Barbara Green and Reinhard Krauss (Minneapolis: Fortress Press, 2003), p. 155.

5. Martin Luther, "Large Catechism: First Part: The Ten Commandments," in Theodore G. Tappert (ed.), *The Book of Concord* (Minneapolis: Fortress Press, 1959), p. 365.

6. John Lahr, "The Player Queen," *New Yorker,* Jan. 21, 2002, p. 62.

7. Dennis Labogin, program manager at Center Point, a substance abuse treatment facility in San Rafael, California, quoted in Peggy Orenstein, "Staying Clean," *New York Times Magazine,* Jan. 10, 2002, p. 39.

## Chapter Six: Forgiveness: Healing and Being Healed

1. Miroslav Volf, *Exclusion and Embrace: A Theological Exploration of Identity, Otherness, and Reconciliation* (Nashville, Tenn.: Abingdon Press, 1996), p. 111.

2. Hannah Arendt, *The Human Condition* (Chicago: University of Chicago Press, 1958), p. 239.

3. Simon Wiesenthal, *The Sunflower* (New York: Schocken Books, 1976).

4. C. S. Lewis, *Letters to Malcolm: Chiefly on Prayer* (Mahwah, N.J.: Paulist Press, 1985), p. 106.

## Chapter Seven: Remembering: Loving with a Resurrection Affection

1. Robert Frost, "The Figure a Poem Makes," *Complete Poems of Robert Frost* (New York: Holt, 1949).

2. Rancher Russell Haasch in an interview with Howard Berkes, "Dying Well in Missoula," *All Things Considered*, National Public Radio, Nov. 6, 1997.

3. Simone Weil, "Forms of the Implicit Love of God," in *Waiting for God*, p. 205.

4. Ron Hansen, *A Stay Against Confusion: Essays on Faith and Fiction* (New York: HarperCollins, 2001), pp. 116–117.

## Chapter Eight: Fidelity: Promising Ourselves Body, Mind, Soul, and Spirit

1. The translator's discretion is admirable. I'm sure Luther used a much earthier word for "the natural movement of the bowels." Martin Luther, "To the Christian Nobility of the German Nation Concerning the Reform of the Christian Estate (1520)," trans. Charles M. Jacobs, in James Atkinson (ed.), *Luther's Works*, vol. 44 (Minneapolis: Fortress Press, 1966), p. 177.

2. Garrison Keillor, "Jim," *News from Lake Wobegon: Spring* (Minneapolis: Minnesota Public Radio, 1983), cassette tape.

3. Margaret A. Farley, *Personal Commitments: Beginning, Keeping, Changing* (San Francisco: HarperSanFrancisco, 1986), p. 34.

4. Wendell Berry, *The Country of Marriage* (Orlando, Fla.: Harcourt Brace, 1973).

5. Augustine, *Confessions*, trans. Henry Chadwick (New York: Oxford University Press, 1991), p. 3.

## Chapter Nine: Practicing Resurrection

1. Wendell Berry, "Manifesto: The Mad Farmer Liberation Front," *Collected Poems, 1957–1982* (San Francisco: North Point Press, 1984), p. 151.

2. I thank Ronald Rohlheiser for the phrase "letting your loss bless you," in *The Holy Longing: The Search for a Christian Spirituality* (New York: Doubleday, 1999), pp. 147, 162 ff.

3. Gerard Manley Hopkins, "Pied Beauty," in *Poetry and Prose*, Walford Davies (ed.) (London: Dent, 1998), p. 48.

# Recommended Reading

Arendt, Hannah. *The Human Condition*. Chicago: University of Chicago Press, 1958.

Augustine. *Confessions* (R. S. Pine-Coffin, trans.). New York: Penguin Classics, 1978.

Bass, Dorothy C. (ed.). *Practicing Our Faith: A Way of Life for a Searching People*. San Francisco: Jossey-Bass, 1997.

Bass, Dorothy C. *Receiving the Day: Christian Practices for Opening the Gift of Time*. San Francisco: Jossey-Bass, 2000.

Benedict. *The Rule of St. Benedict* (Anthony C. Maisel and M. L. Del Mastro, trans.). Garden City, N.Y.: Image Books, 1975.

Berry, Wendell. *The Country of Marriage*. Orlando, Fla.: Harcourt Brace, 1973.

Berry, Wendell. *Collected Poems, 1957–1982*. San Francisco: North Point Press, 1984.

Bondi, Roberta. "Praying the Lord's Prayer: Truthfulness, Intercessory Prayer, and Formation in Love." In E. Byron Anderson and Bruce T. Morrill (eds.), *Liturgy and the Moral Self: Humanity at Full Stretch Before God*. Collegeville, Minn.: Liturgical Press, 1998.

Bondi, Roberta. *To Love as God Loves: Conversations with the Early Church*. Nashville, Tenn.: Abingdon Press, 1996.

Bonhoeffer, Dietrich. *Discipleship* (Barbara Green and Reinhard Krauss, trans.). Minneapolis: Fortress Press, 2003.

Bonhoeffer, Dietrich. *Life Together/Prayerbook of the Bible* (Daniel W. Bloesch and James H. Burtness, trans.). Minneapolis: Fortress Press, 1996.

Borg, Marcus. *Meeting Jesus Again for the First Time*. San Francisco: HarperSan-Francisco, 1994.

Dillard, Annie. *Holy the Firm*. New York: HarperCollins, 1977.

Donahue, John R. *The Gospel in Parable: Metaphor, Narrative, and Theology in the Synoptic Gospels*. Minneapolis: Fortress Press, 1988.

Farley, Margaret A. *Personal Commitments: Beginning, Keeping, Changing*. San Francisco: HarperSanFrancisco, 1986.

Gula, Richard M. *The Good Life: Where Morality and Spirituality Converge*. Mahwah, N.J.: Paulist Press, 1999.

Hansen, Ron. *A Stay Against Confusion: Essays on Faith and Fiction*. New York: HarperCollins, 2001.

Hauerwas, Stanley. "Sex in Public: Toward a Christian Ethic of Sex." In *A Community of Character: Toward a Constructive Christian Social Ethic*. Notre Dame, Ind.: University of Notre Dame Press, 1981.

Hellwig, Monika K. *The Eucharist and the Hunger of the World*. (2nd ed.) Kansas City, Mo.: Sheed & Ward, 1992.

Hopkins, Gerard Manley. *Poetry and Prose*. London: Everyman Paperbacks, 1998.

Keillor, Garrison. "Jim." *News from Lake Wobegon: Spring* [cassette tape]. Minneapolis: Minnesota Public Radio, 1983.

Lewis, C. S. *Letters to Malcolm: Chiefly on Prayer*. Mahwah, N.J.: Paulist Press, 1985.

Luther, Martin. *Luther's Works* (Jaroslav Pelikan, ed.). Saint Louis, Mo.: Concordia, 1955–1986).

Murdoch, Iris. *The Sovereignty of Good*. New York: Routledge, 1970.

Norris, Kathleen. *The Cloister Walk*. New York: Riverhead Books, 1987.

Rohlheiser, Ronald. *The Holy Longing: The Search for a Christian Spirituality*. New York: Doubleday, 1999.

Spohn, William C. *Go and Do Likewise: Jesus and Ethics*. New York: Continuum, 1999.

Volf, Miroslav. *Exclusion and Embrace: A Theological Exploration of Identity, Otherness, and Reconciliation*. Nashville, Tenn.: Abingdon Press, 1996.

Volf, Miroslav, and Bass, Dorothy C. (eds.). *Practicing Theology: Beliefs and Practices in Christian Life*. Grand Rapids, Mich.: Eerdmans, 2002.

Wallace, Catherine M. *For Fidelity*. New York: Alfred A. Knopf, 1998.

Weil, Simone. *Waiting for God* (Emma Craufurd, trans.). New York: HarperCollins, 1951.

Wiesenthal, Simon. *The Sunflower*. New York: Schocken Books, 1976.

Wuthnow, Robert. *After Heaven: Spirituality in America Since the 1950s*. Berkeley: University of California Press, 1998.

# The Author

. . . . . . . . . . . . . . . . . . . . . . . . . . . . . . . . . . . . .

Martha Ellen Stortz is professor of historical theology and ethics at Pacific Lutheran Theological Seminary, an institution affiliated with the Graduate Theological Union in Berkeley, California. She is a layperson in the Evangelical Lutheran Church in America and is widely respected for her speaking and teaching in the church. Author of *PastorPower: Power and Leadership in Ministry* (Abingdon Press, 1993), she has also written numerous articles and chapters in books. She serves on the editorial boards of *Theological Education, Word and World,* and *dialog.* She lives in Oakland, California, with her husband, William C. Spohn.

# Index

# Other Books of Interest

 **Hearing with the Heart: A Gentle Guide to Discerning God's Will for Your Life**
**Debra K. Farrington**
**Hardcover**
**ISBN: 0–7879–5959–6**

"Wise, thoughtful, gentle, honest—Debra Farrington is exactly the kind of companion we are hoping to find to travel with us on our journey home."

—**Robert Benson, author, *The Game: One Man, Nine Innings—A Love Affair with Baseball* and *Between the Dreaming and the Coming True: The Road Home to God***

"Debra K. Farrington knows that finding what to do with our lives—and making courageous and wise decisions at crucial turning points—is a primary need faced by all of us. She offers invaluable guidelines in her highly readable *Hearing with the Heart*."

—**Malcolm Boyd, poet/writer in residence, Episcopal Cathedral Center of St. Paul, and author, *Are You Running with Me, Jesus?***

"The perfect handbook for anyone seeking a direction in life: practical information combined with grace-filled writing and a thorough explanation of the discernment process. Highly recommended reading for church discernment groups."

—**Nora Gallagher, author, *Things Seen and Unseen: A Year Lived in Faith* and *Practicing Resurrection: A Memoir of Discernment***

Only through learning to hear with our hearts tuned closely to God can we discern how we should find our way through the crowded and confusing thickets of our lives. In *Hearing with the Heart*, popular writer and retreat leader Debra Farrington leads you through a gentle process for discovering how to invite God's presence into every aspect of your daily life. Her story-filled discussions of key practices such as prayer, meditation, reading and reflection, and attentiveness to your body, your studies, and your relationships with your friends and family, help you discover how to be open to discerning God's will. Filled with a wealth of exercises, guidelines, and tools, *Hearing with the Heart* gives you the practical help you need to bring you closer to God. As you put these suggestions into practice you will find yourself opening more and more to God's infinite possibilities for you.

The Wisdom Way of Knowing: Reclaiming an
Ancient Tradition to Awaken the Heart
Cynthia Bourgeault
Hardcover
ISBN: 0–7879–6896-X

"Drawing on resources as diverse as Sufism, Benedictine Monasticism, the Gurdjieff Work, and the string theory of modern physics, Cynthia Bourgeault has crafted her own unique vision of the Wisdom way in this very accessible book, nicely balanced between concept and practice."

—Gerald May, senior fellow, Shalem Institute, and author, *Addiction and Grace* and *Will and Spirit*

"The spiritual wisdom and practical suggestions in this lively and beautiful book will be helpful to many who find themselves setting out on the interior journey."

—Bruno Barnhart, a Camaldolese monk and author, *Second Simplicity: The Inner Shape of Christianity*

"Cynthia Bourgeault's book is a valuable contribution to the much-needed reawakening of spiritual practice within a Christian context. Her sincerity, good sense, metaphysical depth, and broad experience make her a source to be trusted."

—Kabir Helminski, Sufi shaikh, the Threshold Society

Grounded in an ancient and precise science of spiritual transformation, the Wisdom tradition offers a deep and sustaining vision in these turbulent times, facilitating personal transformation and a clearer understanding of life's purpose and meaning. In *The Wisdom Way of Knowing*, Cynthia Bourgeault—an Episcopal priest—locates the Wisdom tradition within early Christianity. By deepening our contemplative practice and being intentional about acts of prayerful labor, she shows us how we can understand and exercise a three-centered way of knowing to illuminate truth inaccessible by the mind alone.

**Broken We Kneel: Reflections on Faith and Citizenship**
**Diana Butler Bass**
Hardcover
ISBN: 0–7879–7284–3

"Amid the cacophony of voices responding to 9/11, this book offers a distinctive pastoral voice that combines the passion of faith with a hands-on cherishing of life. The summons of the book is that we forego macho national pride in a moment of brokenness and return to the most elemental truth of suffering love and buoyant faith. Bass's references stretch from a 'Constantinian hangover' to little Emma who knows how to be generous. The reader will find here a sane, grounded invitation to humanness that is broken, but not driven to despair."

—**Walter Brueggemann, professor, Columbia Theological Seminary, and author, *The Prophetic Imagination***

"Since September 11, 2001, our nation has been torn between testy self-doubt and a new self-congratulatory jingoism. In this highly personal book, Diana Butler Bass offers a constructive lament about what has happened to our understandings of citizenship and faith and, in the tradition of Reinhold Niebuhr, calls people of faith to renew their commitment to a vision of prophetic realism. I highly recommend *Broken We Kneel* both for personal reflection and for congregational discussion."

—**Robert Wuthnow, director, Center for the Study of Religion, Princeton University**

"*Broken We Kneel* makes a compelling argument to restore the church to what surely its founders intended: that it be a community of people who practice the discipline of peace-making. Diana Butler Bass has refused to accept the dangerous association of church with militaristic state and instead argues that, in these saber-rattling times, the church must stand with Jesus in his brokenness and courage. She is a real patriot."

—**Nora Gallagher, author, *Practicing Resurrection: A Memoir of Work, Doubt, Discernment, and Moments of Grace***

*Broken We Kneel* is a thoughtful meditation on the relationship between Christian belief and the demands of American citizenship. Drawing on her personal experience as well as her knowledge of American religious history, renowned author Diana Butler Bass examines the highly controversial topic of the relationship between church and state—and between Christian identity and personal patriotism—in America. Detailing how the historic relationship between Christian identity and secular citizenship has been in conflict for centuries, Bass argues that religious nationalism is a dangerous idea in an age of terror.

**Paths to Prayer: Finding Your Own Way to the Presence of God**
**Patricia D. Brown**
**Hardcover**
**ISBN: 0–7879–6565–0**

"Patricia D. Brown writes about prayer with sensitivity, depth, and comprehensiveness. Most of all, she shares out of her considerable experience, which balances her study of various forms of relating to the Divine."

**—Wayne Teasdale, member, Board of Trustees of the Parliament of the World's Religions, and author, A Monk in the World: Cultivating a Spiritual Life**

"In her remarkable new book, Patricia D. Brown tutors us in the spiritual art of prayer. Gentle, practical, and wise—what a wonderful invitation to the spiritual journey. I can't recommend this book highly enough."

**—Lauren Artress, author, Walking a Sacred Path, and canon for special ministries, Grace Cathedral, San Francisco**

"Paths to Prayer is a sensitive exploration of the role of prayer in everyday life. No matter which spiritual or religious path you have chosen, you will benefit from this wonderful book."

**—Larry Dossey, author, Healing Beyond the Body, Prayer Is Good Medicine, and Healing Words**

With step-by-step instructions for over forty ways to pray, this valuable guide contains a wealth of timeless spiritual prayer practices that Christians have used over the last 2,000 years from cultures around the world. Among the prayer practices you'll encounter in this book are the daily office, the prayer shawl, praying with icons, centering prayer, fasting, prayer beads, walking a labyrinth, pilgrimage, anointing for healing, and praying the scriptures. Paths to Prayer offers a whole-person approach to prayer that takes into account each person's individuality and doesn't assume we all relate to God in the same way. A prayer styles self-assessment will help you reflect on your life, your preferences, and your unique way of interacting with the world. Try new dimensions of praying—innovative, searching, relational, and experiential—to deepen your encounter with the divine.